This is a book that will open your heart to a life of self love.

Rev. Nura Loeks
Spiritual Director of Fellowship of Unity

This is a wonderful story that will rekindle the love in your heart while awakening you to a magnificent spiritual adventure that led to the illumination of the author.

If you're lost, hurting and alone, the love and sincerity of this book will revive you and bring you home. Watch as your pain and hurt disappear, to replaced by the serenity and peace of Divine love.

I really enjoyed this book! Tony Kent has touched the heart in all of us who are seeking to end our suffering and find true and everlasting peace.

Robert Jaffe, MD, DD
Director, Jaffe Institute of Spiritual and Medical Healing

If you are someone whose emotional heart is in pain, this book is for you. If you have tried a little bit of a lot of things to help heal this pain and have not had success, this book will open a whole new world of possibility. Bottom line: **If you want peace in your heart,** *My Journey* **will let you know overwhelmingly that this is possible—not only for your heart, but as a way to touch others so they can have peace in their hearts.**

Gail Joyan is a spiritual business healer and coach
with over 30 years' experience in delivering
transformational programs to the corporate sector

In life we all face challenges and hardships. As a practitioner, I am often afforded the opportunity to help. I admire the wisdom within this book. While Tony's touching story is a great inspiration in itself, what I feel is more important is the way he takes a real honest look at himself and his understanding of God, and shares from his heart the deepest truth he has found. **I believe this book can help anyone, and recommend it whole-heartedly to colleagues, friends, and loved ones.**

David Burdette, C.C.N.,C.C.H.

Love, love, and more love kept pouring from the pages. Tony tells this story from his heart to the heart of the reader...to my heart...and I wept.

The narrative style of Tony's writing created the feeling that a gentle dialogue existed between us, and I felt as though I too was a witness to his deep and personal spiritual experiences. *My Journey to Know the Truth* is a hidden jewel longing to be known.

I read Tony's manuscript in one sitting—just a couple hours' easy reading. And then for some reason I was compelled to read it again. And then again! I have read many books in one sitting—a couple hours' easy reading— read them once and never again. There is something divine about the love in this book, and the way Tony delivers it, that keeps calling me back to read it again.

Dr. Ted Fish, Educational Consultant
President, Fish Learning Solutions

Many people search are searching for healing and fulfillment. They dream of meeting a teacher who can take them by the hand and lead them home. Through Tony's story we can share in not only the searching for and finding of that teacher, but also the priceless jewels he received from that relationship.

James Keeley teaches spiritual healing to groups and individuals across the country. He is a principal partner of Lionheart consulting

This book will change your life.

If you are looking for personal healing, spiritual renewal and inspiration, this is the book for you. **Once again, Tony Kent is writing from the heart, sharing his own personal journey of spiritual transformation. This book opens the door of hope for all people.** *My Journey* **will show you how to live with an open, loving heart that swims in the beauty and joy of many divine blessings.**

John Laird, MD, is an integrative medicine
physician specializing for 25 years in the fields of
personal transformation and spiritual healing.

A heartfelt testimony to one man's relationship with his guide—**a touching and vulnerable account of one man's journey to the source of love.** The spirit of his guide breathes through these words, so much that the guide's presence is palpable while you read. This story gives the reader a practical understanding of the teachings, and of how to apply them in your life.

Nura Laird, MEd
http://www.lovingyourfamily.org

I've known Tony Kent for several years, and I have found him to be loving, wise, grounded and humble. He deeply walks his talk. Therefore this text was a relevation... What a tribute to Tony's sincerity and the transformative powers of the teachings he used to create a new life, to ignite the passion and possibility of letting go of one's own private hell. If you are yearning for such completeness, you must read this book.

Patricia Brady
Triathlete, Minister and Adult Educator

My Journey
to Know
the Truth

Healing the Broken Heart

My Journey to Know the Truth
Healing the Broken Heart

Cover illustration and design by:
Marilyn Hager Adleman
http://www.purplefishmedia.com

Cover rose and star concept:
Huda Al Jamal

Edited and typeset by:
Heather Slater
heather@dancingcatcommunications.com

For information on copyright permissions, personal appearances, public speaking, etc., contact the author:

Tony Kent
130 Crane Drive
San Anselmo, CA 94960
www.healingthebrokenheart.com
tony@healingthebrokenheart.com

Outskirts Press
http://www.outskirtspress.com

Outskirts Press and the "OP" logo are trademarks belonging to Outskirts Press, Inc.

Printed in the United States of America

My Journey
to Know
the Truth

Table of Contents

I believe that in order to lead a full life one must not only know God but stay connected to God.

I dedicate this story to my four children—Jessica, Jason, Justin and Tara—because they are without a doubt the most inspirational people I have ever met. They show me each day, in each moment, the divine potential that exists in every one of us. They show me what it is to lead a truthful, meaningful life. They share their hearts openly, honestly, and courageously. I have never, ever not felt their love. I love them totally and completely, and am blessed to have them in my life. They have been instrumental in helping me stay connected to God, and I thank them, their Mom, and God, from the depths of my heart.

I also dedicate this story in loving memory of my Dad, who lives always in my heart, and to my Mom, who has always inspired me with her unconditional love.

Introduction

*H*ave you ever had a broken heart? Have you ever felt abandoned, rejected, deserted or simply not accepted by someone you loved? Have you ever been divorced, a single parent, or simply had a relationship end when you weren't prepared for it to end? Have you been broke or bankrupt, lost a job or been unable to find a job? Have you ever been hurt emotionally, physically or spiritually? Have you ever lost someone you love? Have you questioned your faith—or has it been shattered? Have you had low self-esteem or felt like giving up?

If you answered *yes* to any of these questions, then I think you will find we share a common ground, and you might find some help in this story, just as I did. I was (I thought) a happily married man with four children, living what appeared to be a pretty idyllic life. I was a successful fashion photographer living in Santa Fe, New Mexico, in a wonderful house on over five acres, with a dog, horses, and other household pets. All of us were living healthy and vibrant lives.

I was raised in an upper middle class environment, went to church on Sunday (Episcopalian) and attended private schools, and had traveled much of the world. I had explored all the religions, lived in France for over two decades, worked for most of the top magazines and felt pretty content with myself and my life.

Then everything suddenly changed. My wife, the mother of my four children, went through some powerful changes within herself, and decided it was time to move on. My life was turned upside down, my heart was shattered, my spirit was almost broken. I went through some painful and dark experiences. I found myself alone with my four kids, rendered what felt to be completely dysfunctional by the pain, with no desire to work, and using every ounce of strength I had just to get through each hour. I used up all my life savings, basically gave up photography, and had no idea how I was going to live or what I was going to do. I started seeking different counsel, going from therapists to shamans to Buddhists monks, Christian clergy, Tarot readers, astrologers and psychics, and reading any book I could get my hands on… desperately seeking a solution. I would have stayed with any of the paths, if I felt it offered relief from my pain and solutions to my challenges. One of the main reasons I didn't stay with any of them was that I never met anyone who walked those paths, whom I felt was actually an authentic guide—until I met the man I will introduce to you. I'm not saying there wasn't anyone, just that I never met them; if I did, I did not recognize them. I first embraced the teacher, then the path. So this story is about the man I embraced, and the path I took that brought me to a new life. **This is my journey to know the truth.**

As we are all one heart, one mind, one body, and one soul, I think you may find yourself in this story as well. From my heart to yours, I hope that, in the teachings I found, you will experience some truths that will help heal your heart.

"Pain is a common denominator drawing people together. The greatest pain is separation from God, and drawing nearer to God lessens the pain; because with proximity comes immense relief from pain and immense gratitude fills our being, filling and replacing the void previously experienced." (Quote from my Guide, Sidi)

Prologue

From the spirit of my beloved father the guide, and with his permission, I write these words. For he has said, "Write, with all my blessings. Write for everyone who likes to drink from the source of the love and the peace and the mercy and the justice, through the religion of the unity."

And so I write.

This is a story about love. It is written from love, to love, for love, by love and with love. It is about what I love, whom I love, how I love, why I love and what I have discovered about love. It is mostly about teachings I love from someone I love—someone who has opened my heart to knowing love in a way I never knew existed—and how he, these teachings and this love have changed my life and my self in ways I could never have imagined. And it is about how this person and his teachings guided me to open my wounded heart and be able to love again.

Please know that I am a simple servant who loves God. I am not so much as a drop in the ocean of the heart of my guide and teacher, not so much as a grain of sand in the desert of his vastness, not so much as a piece of dust under his foot. I write to share my heart with you in the hope that you will feel your own heart open to the essence of these teachings and, with this opening, know more about your self and your own journey.

My prayer is that nothing I write here originates with me. These writings and thoughts are simply paraphrases and interpretations of what I have learned and what has been given me. Before I came upon this man and these teachings, I was a truly wandering soul: eternally hungry for some true tasting, drinking from many wells that left me always thirsty, eating from many tables that left me forever hungry.

If God wills, may my words serve as a bridge for you to understand more about these teachings, and how they might be applied to living life in these times. **But reading and studying these teachings is just one part of the walking. Bringing them into your heart and expressing them with love in your life changes everything.** May they help you experience your true nature through the way they work in your life, rather than through an attempt at an intellectual understanding or thought process as they are read. May they stimulate your thought process and open possibilities of expansion for you.

The teachings to which I refer come from God through a man who goes by the name of Sidi Shaykh Muhammad Sa'id Al-Jamal ar-Rifa'I ash-Shaduhuli (may God bless and sanctify his secret). He is known affectionately by his beloveds as Sidi; it is as Sidi that I will mostly refer to him in this book.

When I write and express Sidi's teachings, I have tried to keep everything as he expressed it. His expressions have a different flavor when spoken in his own language and translated into English, than when spoken in English. I have tried not to change his words or phrases, so that the flavor and holiness of his message remains as he expressed it. His expression in English is quite special, and reflects how truly unique he is.

Sidi is the author of over a dozen books, has lived on the Mount of Olives in Jerusalem since 1959, and is a family man with six children. He is, quite simply, not who most people think he is. The path that Sidi teaches, of self-realization through proximity with God, is known as Sufism. Sufism is an ancient mystical tradition that teaches knowledge of God through the purifying and opening of the heart. The steps that are taught to help with this purification are known as stations of the way. Sufism is based on monotheism, the idea that there is only one God, as taught in the three holy scriptures of the original Bible, Torah and Koran. We are taught that it is through love that we can know God.

When I first met Sidi, his teachings were not in book form. They were kept on sheets of paper in his zawiyah (a place of religious retreat) in Jerusalem, and the only way to take any of these teachings away was to spend the necessary time writing them by hand. At that period of his life, Sidi was what is called a "hidden teacher"—he was not easy to find, and had not yet felt permission from God to share himself and what he carries with the world as he does now.

As far as I am concerned, Sidi is still a hidden teacher: Few people are aware of what he carries, or of who he is; many who do know him, know only a small part of him. Can you know the desert from just one grain of sand? Can you know the ocean from just one drop of water? Our experience of Sidi is limited by our own level of understanding and expression. It took me a long time to know even a part of him, so I have chosen to reveal him to you bit by bit as well. Please be patient; let me set the stage a little before you meet him.

When I look at the world, much is hidden from me. This is due to my own limitations and God's good grace for, in His infinite wisdom, He allows me to see only what I am ready to see. In His generosity, He veils me from things I am not ready to experience. **I believe realization is our human birthright; it is a purpose of our existence. Yet, like all things, it comes in stages. These stages are dependent on the inner work we do and our level of preparation.**

Sidi has said that the evolution of the soul is the main and central reason for the existence of the universe. God's entire creation exists as a test and a teaching for the soul. Creation is the cosmic holy book. **With the help of the revealed scriptures and the spiritual disciplines Sidi teaches us, we have a greater chance of connecting with the higher and more luminous parts of humanity.** Throughout the written holy book, we are reminded to contemplate creation—inwardly and outwardly, minutely and cosmically—as a method for developing our spiritual awareness. Just as we witness events in life with various degrees of understanding, holy scripture reveals itself to us in accordance with our state.

If we can imagine the universe in its original state—as a vast and immeasurable expanse of light, with no borders, limits,

2.

1-K-1-1317

Entered Date: 6/6/2022

Entered By: Mee Lor

ISBN: 9781598000849

Condition: Used - Good

Comments: Good Condition.

shape or form—and know that God can shape it with just His will, we can sense the immense power of His love, which brought all of creation into existence. I would imagine that, to Sidi's eye, there is balance and harmony everywhere—that everything is full of spiritual meaning and of this love.

Sidi is still hidden because people are not ready to see; it is no more his decision than ours. Those who do the inner work and study the teachings are able to perceive and understand more, of both Sidi and his teachings. When Sidi addresses our beings, he is not addressing a part of us, but our whole essence—parts of us that he sees, even though we don't. **Our spiritual being is not a small part of our reality; rather, it is the whole of our selves.** So when Sidi talks to us through his teachings, he is addressing all the different levels of our being—those that are known to us, as well as those that are known to him.

If you are like me, you carry many personal preconceptions; you may not even be conscious of some or most of them. It has been my experience that, while in the presence of Sidi— his body or his spirit—I am able to address parts of myself that, until that moment, were hidden from me. These precon- ceptions I have held to, clung to with desperate hope in many cases, have a way of swimming to the surface at the strangest moments. But thankfully, they do surface, so I can deal with them. For example: You might hold an idea of someone, which carries a judgement about that person; this judgement is based on an idea that you hold to be true, because someone told you something that you accepted as truth. However, the statement may not actually be true, so you cannot see clearly who the person truly is. The person may not change at all but, if you change and your perception alters, you will see the person differently.

Love is the basis of all Sidi teaches. What he calls tawid (affirming the unity of God), is the heart and soul of all that I have learned from him. **The secret of the unity is hidden in the love.** He is so constantly occupied with the essential unity of all creation that one cannot help but be aware of this, and it awakens our own desire to experience our origin and the truth of our existence. **Just as God created the world as a manifestation of the endless possibilities of His own limitless and divine being, Sidi manifests for us the endless possibilities of our own greatness and divinity.** When I look at him, I see more of divinity in human form than in anyone else I have ever met. So as I experience him, I experience my own possibilities. The more I love him, the more I love my own potential.

What I marvel at is the possibilities of self-knowledge— because, through Sidi, I feel where the true power lies and how vast the possibilities are.

In one of Sidi's books it is written that God said, "I was a hidden treasure desiring to be known, so I manifested all of creation that I might be known." The hidden treasure was the endless possibilities of existence, all in their unmanifested, undifferentiated states. **Love brought all of creation into being, for God Himself had yearning, a yearning that came from love and manifested in a desire to know Himself. It**

was out of love for the endless possibilities of self-expression that God brought everything from the unseen to the seen. So in this sense creation is a rendering of the invisible into the visible.

This is the divine process I've experienced since being with Sidi. He brings forth from my inner, unseen parts, feelings and emotions I had sensed but was unable to fully realize. This experience of divine creation now issues forth from within me, under his guidance, into fields of visibility and tangible experiences. So in the manner that God's love moved Him to manifest, and bring into existence His creation, Sidi's love moves me to manifest and bring into existence my own true nature. It is as if Sidi wishes to see himself, or an expression of himself, in me. There are times I feel it is not only my yearning to know such things, but his yearning as well. His desire to have me know God draws out my inner nature, which is to know God in a more realized way. **It is from his love that I realize my own love.**

God has said, "Neither my heavens nor my earth contain me, but the heart of my beloved servant contains me." So I ask God that, through my heart and the expression of my heart, Sidi may experience some part of himself, of his own treasure. May a small trace of what he teaches, of what he helps bring into existence, be rendered through this book into the visible world, in a way that satisfies both him and God.

I also pray that these writings may touch a part of your heart, in a way that honors what is highest and noblest and most pure within you, so that more love is expressed and more of God is known and tasted by others. I give deep thanks to Sidi and to God for the chance to share my heart with you, as I know that my heart and yours are the same.

With Sidi as my guide, and with God as my creator and sustainer, I pray that this drop of sharing will add to and merge with the ocean of love that is within us all.

Invitation to a New Creation

*I*f you are reading these words, if you love God, then I am your brother—whether you are black or white, male or female, young or old. **There is no difference between you and me. My story is your story, my love is your love, my heart is your heart. My walking is for you, as well as for me.**

This world, this path, is full of signs. Each manifestation of earthly reality eventually leads to a divine reality. As we grow more aware, we start to understand the signs. Just as a sign pointing to New York might not be significant to someone with no desire to go to New York, certain signs that could lead you to a divine reality have no significance until you become aware that you are seeking it. **Once the desire and the intent to reach the true reality manifest, everything in existence points to that reality.** I know of nothing greater in creation than the human existence, so there is no greater sign of the divine existence than the human being. We are taught on this path that God said, "Know yourself and you will know me."

As we are all one heart, one body, one mind, one soul…if you can understand me, you can understand yourself. So I will ask God to help me bare my very existence and reveal my innermost heart, so that we can come to an understanding that leads us to a deeper knowing of Him.

The heart is our innermost consciousness; it is the place where God has hidden His secret. The teachings say that God has said: "I have hid this secret in the heart of my beloved slave, but he must destroy the mountain of his existence to know this secret." As the heart is the place of enthronement, so it is also the place where the lover of God recognizes himself. Our way, the Shaddhuli way, is about knowledge of God through the heart—specifically, through the opening of the heart and the release of the love that is both our origin and our destination. **The mind, in all its magnificence, cannot know God. Only the heart can know God.**

When the heart opens and love flows unconditionally, we live as extensions of God, who loves unconditionally. God created us from His love and graced us with love, so that we may use this love to return to our origin. It is through an outpouring of unconditional love that one finds peace; for without this outflow of love, there is no real peace.

When our love is blocked, we experience pain—and there is nothing more painful than blocked love. People often think they experience pain because they are not receiving the love they seek, when the real source of the pain is their own blocked love. We were created to be a natural extension of divine love, so when we close our heart to this love, we do not live in the flow of who we were created to be.

When I went through a painful separation from my wife of over 20 years, the mother of my four children, I was convinced the pain I felt came from the fact that she had stopped giving me the love I sought. I was so hung up on getting the love from a particular face, that I could not experience the joy of others' love. This period lasted for more than four years, and was probably the saddest and most depressing time of my life. By the same token, it provoked such an immense spiritual crisis that it led me, out of desperation, to the heart of Sidi and to his teachings. It is the catalyst for this story. I still marvel at God's infinite wisdom and compassion.

People often ask Sidi questions, such as *What is evil? Where does it come from? Why does it exist?* If I were to condense all his answers that I've seen, heard or read about this question, into a simple statement that applies to life in the material world, I would say that evil is actually blocked love. Was it not blocked love that allowed Hitler to do what he did? **Blocked love creates almost all the pain we feel and see people experiencing in the world.**

Blocked love is the cause and origin of my story with Sidi. It was when my heart shut down, when the immense pain of blocked love so overwhelmed me, when I became almost totally dysfunctional, that I was finally driven from within to reach out for help. **Evil happens when good people do nothing.** Even small acts can make a big difference. Dripping water will fill a glass, one drop at a time.

There could never be just the absence of love. Love is always present, though not always expressed. Love is eternal; it is the power behind creation. It is, has been, and always will be present. When I refer to the absence of love, it will always be in the sense that there is an absence of the outpouring or expression of love—this is what I refer to as "blocked" love. If all of our personality was removed from what is happening, we would exist in a pure state of love; in this pure state, love would flow from our hearts as a pure release of divine energy. It is our personality that complicates and distorts the expression of love, and many of Sidi's teachings are based on how to correct this situation—to do what Sufis call "cleaning the nafs."

When people begin studying Sidi's teachings, there is often quite a bit of confusion about the nafs: *What is the nafs? What does this word refer to?* (At least this was the case for me.) It is a large, multi-dimensional word, which has different meanings depending on where and how it is used. Nafs is an Arabic word and, though it ends with the letter *s* in English, it is a singular noun. Sometimes "the nafs" refers to the soul, as does the Latin expression *anima,* or the Greek *psyche.* The nafs, as I have come to understand it and will refer to it in this story, is one's self—i.e., our personality traits, the more intellectual part of our being—and will be referenced as an undeveloped state.

There is a connection through the nafs to the material world. As Sidi explains, the nafs comes from your self: your perception, your hearing, your feeling, all those voices you hear in your mind, and the desires you feel in your heart. Our nafs gets excited by desires and material wishes and, in turn, excites us to want things. People often measure their level of attainment by the number of things they acquire. I used to do this myself. **I feel now that the things we remember most in life are not things, but experiences. Sidi has told me again and again not to love things that don't love back.**

I remember when I first heard Sidi's voice. That is, I remember the experience, though not the date or day. I was in New York City, where I had gone to work. I was a photographer at the time, and was doing a shoot there. I was in a hotel room, feeling particularly depressed. My life had totally—and to me, inexplicably—fallen apart. My marriage was unstable, my wife was seeing other men, and I felt lost and powerless. It was as if I was heading over a cliff and couldn't stop it from happening. I had a constant, nagging pain in my gut. I was so stressed, so tense and nervous, that I had severe intestinal cramps and massive heartburn. I couldn't sleep or eat, and was quite desperate. Yet I was absolutely convinced that, if my wife loved me again, all would be well. So in essence, I blamed her for all my misery.

I had been going through a lot of counseling, and one of the couples I had been working with, Nura and Tarik Loeks, had known Sidi for a number of years. Nura had given me Sidi's phone number in Jerusalem, but I had not yet worked up the courage to call. However, this particular time in New York , I was so depressed and desperate that I decided to make the call. Working with Nura, I had come to the conclusion that I was experiencing a spiritual crisis, even more than an emotional upheaval. She had talked with Sidi about my situation, and Sidi had told her to have me call him.

Often in life, we are offered solutions to difficult challenges but, because of veils that are placed between us and the solution, we remain stuck in our situations until the time is right for movement. Either our pain becomes so overwhelming that we simply cannot stay in that station any more, or the call of a more positive feeling beckons us forward. In my case, the pain was the motivating factor: I was so depressed that I saw nothing positive in the future. I was reading books like *When Bad Things Happen to Good People* (Kushner, 1983), and feeling pretty sorry for myself.

I believe God constantly surrounds us with doorways and solutions that we don't recognize. I don't think I recognized all the gifts coming to me, though the Loeks were certainly one, and the opportunity to meet Sidi was definitely another.

So I was sitting in a hotel room, on a bed, facing the other bed in the room. I had the telephone in my hand, and it felt like it weighed 500 pounds. I make my living calling strangers on the phone and sharing a home-based business opportunity with them, so I'm accustomed to talking on the phone. But my state of mind then was predominantly sad and fearful. **Fear is an absence of love and lack of faith.**

There was a part of me that said, *If this doesn't work, then what?* I felt this may be my last chance because, if Sidi could not help—and I think that, in my mind, I felt he couldn't—I would be totally lost. I had no way of consciously knowing that I was about to experience one of the major turning points of my life.

I have often considered that thought. What if I had not made that call? Where would my life be today? What direction would I have gone? Whom would I have become? **How would my life have been different if I had made a different choice in that moment?** As I explore this moment in the hotel room, and before moving on with my story, I want to take you back a bit in my life. Life-changing moments, such as the one I was about to experience, probably have their beginnings in some other moment, which might pass unnoticed. I have spent considerable time thinking about certain life-defining moments, and trying to work my way back to how I got on a particular path. **It is true that, at times, seemingly trivial or inconsequential acts can change our lives dramatically. This story is about such moments.**

One day, maybe six months before I sat in that New York hotel room, I was walking down the hallway of a rather large house that I owned and was living in. I was headed toward the children's rooms, when their phone rang. I don't think I had picked up their phone once in the year before that call—but that day I did. It was a friend, calling to ask my oldest daughter, Jessica, to babysit. She happened to ask how I was; I told her I was not well, that I was depressed and in a lot of pain. I mentioned I had seen a number of people for counseling but didn't feel I was making progress, because I felt I was having more of a spiritual crisis than an emotional one.

I didn't know this friend, Adrianna, that well. But I was at a point in my life when I would talk to anyone who would listen; mostly, I complained about my situation and expressed anger toward my wife. So it was not unusual that I would share intimate information with someone I didn't know well.

"I know just the person for you," Adrianna said, and told me to call Nura Loeks. She said that Nura focused completely on the spiritual essence of things, and would be the perfect person to help me. And when I hung up I actually did just that: I called Nura. To this day, I believe Nura was sent by God to help me move toward healing. She eventually led me to Sidi.

When I go further back into my memory, I can trace more of the lines of my life that led to that moment in that hotel room. I remember stopping for lunch with my kids in a little restaurant in Santa Fe. It was there, seemingly by accident, that we had met Adrianna. She happened to be sitting next to our table, and she had a little girl with her who kept smiling at us, so we struck up a conversation. It turned out that her husband was into horses, was in fact a gold medal Olympic champion. Jessica has a passion for horses. Soon, Adrianna was asking her to babysit; eventually, Jessica even traveled with them to help with their daughter, Ruby, while Adrianna's husband rode in horse shows.

And so I wondered: If I had not met Adrianna at that restaurant, and if I had not picked up the kids' phone— would I have met Nura and Sidi? I feel it was my destiny to know Sidi and that, one way or another, it would have happened. **But it is still interesting to look at the outcomes of seemingly happenstance moments, and to see how a single moment can change your life forever.**

I know now that my wife meeting other men was also pivotal in driving me to my destiny—and that behind each moment and every veil, there is the deep wisdom of God. Just as a car will not function without its key, though the key is only a small part of the whole, I have realized that small and seemingly unimportant instances can radically change the direction of our lives. **And since our destinies can be so radically altered in any given moment, it makes sense to be present and aware in every moment.**

Sometimes we feel the need to make big changes in our lives in order to have a different outcome. It is said, "Do what you've always done and you'll get what you always gotten." Look at it this way: If you start walking in a straight line toward a certain place, and then take one small turn to the right or left, you will end up in a completely different place than planned. And the longer you walk, the farther you will move from the original direction. **A small change in direction, by the end of a lifetime, can mean you end up in a completely different place—far indeed from where you were originally headed.**

Sidi never relents for a moment in his teaching about being the "son or daughter of your moment." He can collapse time frames like no one I have ever met because he simply never, ever tolerates procrastination. Yet it is amazing how much patience he is capable of when the moment calls for it. I have spent a lot of time learning when to take action and when to be patient. **One of the things I've learned is that, when I need to take action to create something, I must be the "son**

of my moment." And I can use patience when waiting for things beyond my control to develop.

So in the last several years I have learned to pay much closer attention to the moment, knowing that it is a microcosm of my world. I started this book months before writing the words you are reading now but, because I was finishing another book, I have procrastinated on this one. However, I am not comfortable with this fact because, once Sidi said to write, I should have continued to write. **I wanted to write this book, and when you really want to do something, you find a way. If you don't want to do something, you find excuses.** But don't confuse activity with achievement. Just being busy doesn't mean you are advancing towards the realization of a goal. The activity must be focused and, in my opinion, done with joy. **When I start to create or build something I imagine very strongly that I am in love with the result, and I know I am on track when I am happy and it feels good.**

Our emotions are a tremendous barometer. Divine love permeates every single part of the universe and flows through everything that exists. Whether you choose to accept it or resist it, the love is always there. In order to drink from this stream of divine love and receive its blessings, we must be in harmony with the flow. If you resist the love, you are unable to receive it. Our emotions let us know if we are accepting or resisting this love. **The better you feel, the more you are open to allowing divine love to flow through you; the worse you feel, the less you are allowing this connection.** We can choose to allow divine love to flow through us; when we do so, we allow a fuller connection with God to express itself, and this is a joyful feeling. This well-being is what God intended for us because he created us with divine love.

Sidi taught me that my feelings of insecurity, frustration, pain and anger were due to a disconnection with this divine love. Through prayer and remembrance you can intentionally reach for thoughts that will hold you in a vibrational harmony with who you really are; then things will start to flow in a positive direction. When two people both face God, they could not intentionally do something to hurt each other. This only happens when one or the other feels disconnected.

I have studied the work of a writer named Robert Fritz, who is a master at teaching people how "creative avoidance" can infringe upon one's life, sometimes to such a degree that we can be stuck forever in a similar place. He writes about creative/advancing structures and conflicting/oscillating structures; he states that, if we want to change our outcomes, we have to change the structure of our lives. **Energy will always move along the path of least resistance. If we want to change the way water flows through nature, we have to change the river bed. If we want to change the direction we are moving in our lives, we must make structural changes.**

There are three basic insights in Fritz's teachings: The first is that energy moves along the path of least resistance. The second is that the underlying structure of your life determines the path of least resistance. The third is that you can change the fundamental underlying structures of your life.

So there I was, sitting in a hotel room—pain in my heart, pain in my gut, full of fear, sadness, desperation and other troubling emotions. I could identify, and even name, most of my painful thoughts and feelings, but was unable to treat or cure them. In my soul, it felt like it was late on a dark night. But in New York City, it was just late on a Saturday morning. The time in Jerusalem was evening, so I decided to make the call.

I was far too depressed and worried about my life to procrastinate much more. I had spent much of my adult life seeking out and working with spiritual teachers, and had been intimately involved with many of them, so I was not fearful of being able to have a dialogue. I was well trained. In fact, I had been quite close to a Moroccan Sufi for many years, and had spent a lot of time alone with him. But in no way was I consciously aware of the immense spiritual energy I was about to encounter.

Looking back, I have come to the conclusion that Sidi actually drew me to him, and it was more his power reaching out to me than my own initiative. There are many references in his teachings to the way God calls us. And though my mind was too obsessed with my nafs, I am sure my inner, deep heart could feel the pulling. So I called the number and, before I could even gather my thoughts, I heard his voice for the first time. I didn't need to ask if he was there, but I did.

"Hello," I said. "Is Sidi there?"

Nam (yes).

"This is Tony Kent, Sidi, and Nura Loeks gave me your number," I mumbled.

Yes, my beloved. I have been waiting for you.

"I'm in trouble, Sidi," I said. "I need help."

I can see that. Allah is with you.

"I can't feel His presence, Sidi. All I can feel is the pain. I don't know what to do."

Come. I am waiting for you.

"What do you mean? When should I come, Sidi?"

Now. This is your time.

It seemed like a lifetime passed in the silence that followed. Maybe, in a sense, it did. I didn't know what to say, so I said nothing. **And Sidi waited and held me in the silence, and I had the first taste of his patience and the first feeling of how he could hold my heart.**

I took a deep breath and, feeling insecure, asked, "How soon do you mean, Sidi?" I thought he meant a few weeks, maybe even a few months.

Now. Come now.

"I have four children that I can't leave alone." (My wife was going to Nashville to visit a man she was involved with, and I had no live-in help.) "My wife has left me, and I don't know what to do."

Trust Allah. He cares more about you than you care about yourself.

"How do I get to you?" I asked, more at a loss of words than anything else. "How do I find you?"

Come to Tel Aviv, and then take a taxi to Jerusalem. When you get to Jerusalem, get in a different taxi and tell him, "Take me to Sidi's house." Everyone knows me here.

I was dumfounded. Years ago, during my photography career, I worked in Paris. One day Ahmad, my Sufi friend from Morocco—who had never been out of Morocco—got on a plane and came to Paris without my phone number or address. He got in a taxi at Orly Airport and said to the driver, "Take me to Tony's house."

"Who is Tony?" asked the driver.

"An American photographer with frizzy hair," said Ahmad.

"I know that guy," said the driver, and brought him directly to me. The driver happened to start his evening shift all the time at a stand I often called to pick up models working in my studio. I would always walk them out and give the driver an address, because many of the models didn't speak French. So he recognized me from Ahmad's description.

"What's your address?" I asked Sidi.

You won't need it. All the taxis know me.

Coincidence or not?...I was wondering. I believe it was an intentional, deliberate and deep-seeing message for me. I later learned that most taxis out of Tel Aviv are driven by Jews so, by switching taxis in Jerusalem, I would be with an Arab, who would most likely be Muslim. Since Sidi is the teacher at the complex of al-Aqsa Mosque, he speaks to hundreds of thousands of people there; he is known for helping the poor, and is often on television, so he is well-known, especially by Arab Muslims.

When I finally got to Jerusalem, it was late at night, and it was as cold outside as I felt inside. In the old part of Jerusalem, I got out of the taxi that had taken me from Tel Aviv. As I got into the next taxi, I asked the driver to "take me to Sidi's house." He replied, "Who is Sidi?"

I didn't know how to describe him, as I had never even seen a picture of him, though I had no doubt this was a lesson in trust. I also didn't know much about him, or that he was known at the mosque; in fact, I knew very little about him. I told the driver Sidi had said that all the taxi drivers would know who he was, and suggested driving until we saw another taxi. The first taxi driver we saw did know who Sidi was, and gave my driver directions.

When I finally got to Sidi's house, it was getting much later. I found myself standing in front of a house, alone with my suitcase, not sure I was at the right place—and, as it was dark, I didn't feel I should knock on the door. I was getting cold, and hoping someone would walk by so that I could ask if I was at the right place. I even started to question the wisdom of coming to Jerusalem, and the darkness that had been manifesting inside me started to make itself known again. When one is spiritually fragile, it is hard to think clearly. Before I could figure out what to do, the front door opened.

There stood Sidi. In that moment, as he opened the door, it felt as if he had opened his heart, and something inside my heart knew I had come to a place where I could finally feel safe. He stood as a shadow framed in the light—a clear message that I would only be able to know a certain part of him, and that a lot of him would remain hidden from me.

At that time he was living in what I would call "the old zawiyah." (He now lives in a different house.) We immediately walked down some steps, and entered what became a sanctuary for me...a place where, in a short time, my whole life would change forever. We were met by Maryam, an English lady who had been a student of Sidi's for years. She had obviously also been awaiting my arrival and, after welcoming me warmly, led us inside. There was a mattress on the floor, where Sidi sat; I sat on the floor in front of him as Maryam went to make tea. I later learned Sidi almost always sat on mattresses on the floor, and slept there as well, because that was how the prophet Muhammad, may peace and blessings be upon him, sat and slept. **Sidi carries the bloodline of the Prophet, may peace and blessings be upon him, as well as the teachings and many of the blessings that come from this holy tradition.**

It has been many years since that night but, as I go back in time to share the story with you, the memories are coming back to me. Sidi has always taught me to live in the present, to not look backwards. So I haven't relived these memories often, except when someone asks how I met Sidi, and that is not often. I even taped many of our conversations because, in my confused state during that time, I had so much difficulty hearing what he was telling me. I taped the conversations in desperation, trying to understand. I didn't realize at the time that I was simply resistant to what he said, and to moving forward with it, because I wanted the outcome to be different than the reality I was experiencing.

I have made the decision to write now from memory rather than from the tapes. What is truly important is what I did with what he taught me, and where I went with the guidance he provided. I can't go back and change the way I did things, so going back to the tapes does not seem to have great value. Even if I heard what he shared with me differently now, what has happened is done. One of the main purposes of this story is to share how I adapted and made use of what I consciously remember Sidi teaching me; it isn't about what I didn't assimilate. I now have access to all of Sidi's teachings in the books that have been published, which are consistent with what he told me then and what he tells people today. In fact, there are more secrets revealed now than ever before.

So here it was, just a few hours from morning, and I hadn't slept in a long time. In fact, I hadn't slept well for months, so I was pretty exhausted—which I think was a good thing, in that my defensive nature was down and I was feeling desperate. There was little small talk. Sidi could quite clearly see the station I was in. Unfortunately, I could not say the same, as I was only able to see a tiny part of him. **Even after all these years, I realize that I only know a portion of who he is, but the portion I know has totally captured my heart. As I practice the disciplines and follow the path, every once in a while I feel that I see another dimension of Sidi—as if I were living in a huge house, and every few years I get to see a new room I have never visited before.**

At one time, I had lived in India and studied Sitar. For hours on end, I would practice scales, sometimes to a particular rhythm. After months of practicing a certain scale and a certain rhythm, I could recognize that scale and rhythm when listening to a raga. And sometimes now, when I plunge into one of Sidi's teachings, a similar thing happens. I start to see deeper into the teaching and, as I grow more familiar with what he shares, I experience another dimension of him, and the ways his teachings can help me understand my life.

As I got a bit more relaxed, the questions started pouring from my heart. Sidi took Maryam's hand, wrote some Koranic phrases on it, and then he called the angels through her to answer my questions. Almost all the questions were about my wife. *Why did this happen? Would she come back? What could I do? How were the children? What could I do? Did she really love someone else? What could I do, what could I do, what could I do?*

In my pain and loneliness, I was hoping beyond hope that Sidi would be able to bring my heart some answers I could live with. I am sure that, in his wisdom, he gave me answers that would take me to the limit of my containment. And I am sure he saw that my wife and I would eventually separate and divorce—but as I was in no condition to contain such an answer, he only gave me what my heart *could* contain. So what I remember from that meeting is that there was still hope she would come back. It is entirely possible that, at that moment, this possibility was still a strong one. But my subsequent behavior was such that this never happened. I was so absorbed in her faults that I wasn't looking at my own. **Sidi has taught me that there is no greater fault than being conscious of or absorbed in another's faults,** but I thought the best defense was a strong offense, so I was on the attack. Sidi writes in *Music of the Soul:*

> *You only truly love when you want for your brother or sister what you want for yourself. Be like the candle that burns itself for the sake of giving its light to those around it. This signifies the real love. As a human being we can do*

much more, because we are the ones that carry all the manifestations and projections, the only one who carries them all, of God's qualities in Himself. And this is what makes us so sacred.

And he has said, "Allah made male and female from one soul. In the dictionary of Allah there is no segregation. It is selfish people that follow their egos."

I was angry and hurt, and the dysfunction this caused didn't let me see what I was doing to contribute to these happenings in my life. At the time, I felt everything was her fault, and that I had little to do with it. I was not yet ready to accept my responsibility.

Looking back, I realize there were probably many times when, had I changed, we could have worked things out. But I was doing little to entice her to return. Sometimes I sat by the phone for days, waiting for her to call. When she finally did, I allowed my pain and frustration to take command; I yelled at her, or made her feel guilty for abandoning the kids and me. I can see now why she wouldn't want to come back to such an atmosphere, but at the time I was dominated by my nafs.

So that first evening in Jerusalem, it probably mattered little what Sidi actually said—I was not ready to hear the truth. What was impactful was what he did, and how he contained me. **The overwhelming compassion of his heart and the manner in which he made me feel accepted had great consequence in my life. Even today, there are nuances to**

what Sidi says and how he says it that I don't catch at the moment of expression. But I am learning of the infinite depths beneath and behind everything he says and does.

As I go back in time, searching my feelings and remembering that evening, it feels as if I'm witnessing another life, and I'm having difficulty connecting the dots of the current one with the one back then. I was unstable, so immature in many ways. I realize now that, in reality, I was "cooking." I was cooking to a point where I was tender and ready to be consumed—and consumed I was by the presence of the guide Sidi. Little did I know, I was not even close to finishing my descent into the darkness of my nafs; the pain I felt then was nothing compared to what was to come. But I will never forget how special that evening was. Its fragrance lingers on, even today.

At one point that evening, after Sidi had taken my heart in his, I took his hand and took the promise—the bayat, as we call it—with him. And he gave me the name Salih, which I still carry today. The bayat is a promise made to God, through the spiritual master. When we make the promise to God through the hand of the guide, we promise to follow Him and obey Him; as we do so, we receive a key that helps us return to the real life He created for us from the beginning. We promise to carry the message of the peace and the love and the mercy and the justice. We surrender to the guide, who has himself surrendered to Allah; this is an early stage of our own eventual surrender to God. It is important to know that the guide operates in many worlds that are not seen, well beyond the structures of normal life as we know and experience it. The guide is the living archetype of inspiration.

After taking the promise, I sat on the floor in front of him, and he lay on the mattress with his head resting on his hand, as he frequently does. His eyes were closed and he was traveling with his spirit, and I had an experience that feels as strong today as it did then. As I looked at his face, it seemed to constantly change shape and form. For one moment, I saw him as a dark-skinned, white-bearded, thin and aquiline presence; then I saw him with a whiter face and black beard. Then he took on other countenances that were biblical in feel, but unrecognizable in form. Each had the aura of a spiritual countenance, and each was unique.

And then, as I sat and stared in amazement, I started to feel panic overtake me. It was as if my mind and heart were taken over by a force I could not control, and I felt an immense, uncontrollable fear. What I remember most was worrying what would happen if I saw Sidi the next day: Would I even recognize him? Because, for the life of me, I couldn't find the expression of what he looked like. I think he was showing me certain aspects of his awareness. Looking back, it seems he was also showing me the faces and qualities of different prophets but, instead of being able to sit with it and contain it, I was overwhelmed by my fear. I couldn't stop thinking that, when I saw him again, I wouldn't recognize him. This thought grabbed me in my gut and wouldn't let go, and it started to become an obsession. I could not get a grip on where my mind was going. I felt paralyzed. All my insecurities came to the surface, and I felt terribly threatened. I wasn't just scared—I was terrified.

I can imagine this might seem a bit foolish to you, and I still wonder about it myself. I had practiced meditation and prayer for years, and thought I had a fairly developed spiritual awareness that I could call on in moments that challenged me. But that night with Sidi, I felt childlike and humiliated. It was like being on a bad acid trip, and losing control. I wanted to turn, to look at Maryam, but I couldn't move my eyes from Sidi. The more faces I saw, the more control I lost, and the more deeply and profoundly I experienced the fear.

It turned out to be only a brief preview of what was to come, and the annihilation I would have to go through to walk with his teachings. I started trying to take deep breaths, because it felt as if my breath had stopped. I wanted to move into a different position because my legs were hurting, but I couldn't move. I was paralyzed. I see now that it was a reflection of how paralyzed I had become in my life.

I don't know how long I stayed like that, but it felt like a lifetime. It certainly reflected the impotency I felt. I had felt threatened by the fact that my wife was with other men, and for the longest time I was unable to be close to a woman, either emotionally or physically. Any hint of sexual intimacy brought much sadness for me, and any time I was close to another woman, my thoughts and feelings were in conflict with those for my wife. In the zawiyah, I still wanted to turn, to catch Maryam's attention, hoping she could help me. But I was literally and figuratively transfixed, and all I could do was be in the moment.

What a teaching that was, as I think about it now, but I didn't get it at the time. I was living almost entirely in fear, and it was focused on the future: *Would she come back? Did she still love me? Was there any chance her heart would open to mine again? How could I live without her? What would happen to my children? Would the pain ever go away?* Each thought was directed outside of my self, and concerned with some projected and imagined future event. Only later would I learn more about what Sidi meant when he said to "be the son of your moment."

As I've already mentioned, it was late, and I had not slept for days. Lack of sleep over prolonged periods can definitely wear you down—but it also creates a tiredness so profound that your natural defenses (or systems of creative avoidance) are broken down. I did not have the strength to resist a breakdown any more, and I could feel it coming. I could come up with no clever manipulations to create an illusion, for myself or others, that I was alright.

The feeling reminded me of an experience I had back in Santa Fe, while on my way to a therapist's appointment. I had been to the office many times before, and Santa Fe is not a large town. On this day, I stopped at a red light—and suddenly couldn't remember where the office was. I just went blank, and then got so nervous that I became disoriented. I was actually scared that I was going crazy.

And as I sat before Sidi in the zawiyah, the most positive thought I had was that, if I was losing it, I had certainly come into the presence of someone who could help me. I recalled all the things Nura had told me about Sidi; she was one person I trusted, and probably the closest friend I had at the time. I owe her so much for the love she showed, the infinite patience, and the doorway she helped to open.

I can't remember now how I moved from that station, but the next thing I remember of my first night in Jerusalem is Maryam showing me a bed. Next to the bed was a huge pile of papers; she said these were Sidi's teachings, and that I should not only read them but start to hand copy them onto some paper that she gave me. This was one of the ways Sidi taught. At that time there were no published books, but everything had been typed, mostly by Maryam, I think, on extra-large sheets of paper. She said these papers never left the zawiyah, and all I could take home with me was what I could copy by hand. This fact did not impact me strongly at that moment, because I had not yet read anything.

I could feel the warmth, kindness and caring, the love and tender compassion of Maryam, as she gently held me and said, "Not to worry. Trust Allah and pay close attention to everything with Sidi." And she left me alone, in a simple room with a bed that was on the floor, a table and the teachings. I don't think I had ever felt so alone in my life.

For many years I had sought to know God and, had you asked before this all started, I would have told you I felt close to God—that I loved and trusted and felt aware of God. However, by the time I got to Jerusalem, I could no longer say that. When I prayed, I felt nothing; when I meditated, I could think only of my wife. The biggest challenge was trying to shut off the dark pictures that kept coming to me: pictures of her, joyful, with other men, having great sex...not thinking of me at all. I felt that God had put me in a great garden—Sidi describes it as the paradise of the presence of the unity of God—but somehow I had screwed up. And though I thought I was willing to serve God and give all that God asked, I now realize I held back much that was important. It was as if I offered to share an apple with a starving person, rather than give him the whole apple. *Music of the Soul* says: **Generosity is not in giving a person that which they need more than you; it is in giving them that which you need more than they do.** I don't think we are remembered or honored for what we have received or acquired in life nearly as much as we are revered for what we gave.

As I relive that night, I vividly remember, as tired as I was, picking up the teachings to look through them. One subject after another caught my eye, and I started to panic again. I thought there was no way to read all of them in the time I had, and they all looked so inspiring, and insightful. All the 28 stations were there—*The Secret of the Love, The Story of Adam, Who Are You, The Light of God, The Divine Flute, The Divine Existence, How Do I Speak to My God, The Knowledge of the Sufi Path, The Remembrance*. (All 28 stations are found in Sidi's *Music of the Soul*; information at the end of this book.) They went on and on...I didn't know where to start, and worried that I would never finish. Through my entire stay there, I worried about that. And I learned from it how dissatisfied I was with things, even precious things, that were given to me. I always wanted more. I was definitely not the son of my moment.

I finally chose *The Secret of the Love* because the title attracted me, and I started to read. At the first words, I knew I had found what I'd been seeking for years. From India to Morocco, from Europe to the United States, **I had spent years seeking a guide who was complete as a guide. Along the way I met many great teachers, but I had never met someone I felt was truly realized and complete.** As I read through the first of Sidi's teachings, my heart softened to a point I had never experienced. Not even while making love had I been touched so deeply; never had the beauty and poetry of words affected me so profoundly. I had read and studied many Sufi mystics, but the fact that I had actually met Sidi and was in his presence made everything feel different this time.

My heart felt so tender that I started to cry, first softly and then from a deeper place—a true wudu, or washing and cleansing of my being. But this was a different kind of crying: I cried for all the years I had been wandering, for not getting here earlier. I cried because I wished my wife and kids were here, so I could share with them the radiant truths I was experiencing. I cried from a fullness of love I had never tasted before. I cried for all the things I had done wrong and the hearts I had hurt. I didn't know it at the time, but I was entering the early phases of the station at-tawba (repentance), and it would continue for much longer than that one night.

And so in this special land, where all the prophets walked and taught, I began the journey of a new creation. But first, I had a lot more to go through, a lot more pictures to break. In the cold of a winter night in the city at the heart of the world, I started to discover and feel new things about my heart.

I finally fell asleep, my body unable to resist anymore. But, as I had hardly slept more than a few hours at a time over the preceding months, this night was no different. I was awake again almost before I felt I was asleep. Normally, when going from the U.S. to Europe or to the Middle East, the time zone difference creates challenges with sleep and leaves one feeling tired. Yet even with jet lag, I could not sleep for what felt like any decent length of time.

But this time I woke up with something I wanted to do. So without even leaving the bed, I grabbed the teachings and started to read more. My nafs immediately got involved: I started to worry about which teachings to read first, and which to copy—and before I even got started, I was in a troubled state of mind again. As the fear became dominant, I succumbed to the sadness of my heart, and was over-whelmed with depressing thoughts.

I reached for one of the titles and found myself with *The Story of Adam.* I started reading. I wish I could share more explicitly what it felt like to be full of so many conflicting thoughts and feelings. **Part of me felt bliss from the inner knowing that I was reading words and thoughts that were, without doubt,**

sourced from a place of deep truth and pure knowing. But at the same time, there was a profound sadness as I realized and came to terms with my own ineptitude and lack of knowing.

As I read more of the story of Adam, the contrast between sadness and joy became more and more evident. I started worrying about all the years I had lost reading and studying books that, as I read these teachings, seemed rather inconsequential. Instead of relaxing into the comfort of what I had found, my mind was dominated by thoughts of how stupid I was. Instead of being grateful for what was being given, I was fearful of what I had lost. And instead of just absorbing the answers, I became filled with questions.

As I look back at this time from where I am now, I admit that one of my biggest worries for years was bothering Sidi with the same questions again and again. His infinite patience is a lesson even today. I still find myself getting impatient with people that ask the same question repeatedly. **I think his patience comes from his compassion and the unconditional love he offers everyone. I also believe, as Sidi teaches, that preferring the well-being of someone else over yourself is an essential part of being able to open your heart—and he seems to care more about some of his beloveds than they care about themselves.**

My self-esteem was at an all time low. I had no confidence in my ability to work my way out of the pain I was in, and desperation dominated my thoughts every day.

Sidi had a magical way of making me feel I was important, that he knew everything about me. Even with all the foolish choices and thoughts that dominated my life, he saw value in me. It was through his eyes and heart that I first saw glimpses of the treasures within me, the treasures that every living thing has within.

During the time of my visit in Jerusalem, many questions surfaced that I was too scared to ask. I realize now that I didn't totally want to know the answers. I wasn't ready for all the truth. Allah, in His infinite mercy, protects us by placing veils between us and certain truths, until we are ready to receive these truths. Sidi is a master at knowing just how much we can handle; through the generosity of his love, he gently guides us, by not showing us too much too quickly. Today, there are still things about myself for which I feel shame, and I will deal with them as I become ready. **This is why the prayers, and the studying, and the disciplines are so important: They strengthen the container of our being, so that more truth may be revealed. They bring the limbs to conform through opening the heart to God.**

I also have to admit that I was embarrassed to ask many questions because they came from a part of me I didn't like. Sometimes I would frame a question in such a way that there would be a greater chance of receiving an answer that would feed a hungry nafs. **As I have learned over the years, Sidi may give an answer that can have many different meanings, unless you ask specific questions.**

Let me give you an example. Not that long ago, I bought a house in Santa Fe. It shared a driveway with another house but had a separate title. These houses were in town, by the rail yard, on a street that is being greatly improved and built up. There were more old, unrenovated houses than new houses on the street, but I liked the area and saw great potential. So I put an offer on the house; it was accepted, and I was happy. The house behind it was not for sale, but it was run-down. I thought that, even if I renovated the front house, the value would be hurt because of the condition of the house behind, which in essence shared the same lot. There was an old wooden fence, falling apart, which separated the two properties. So I asked the realtor to find out if there was any way to buy the second house as well. I knew this would overextend me a bit financially, but I felt I could combine the two properties into one, sell them together, and turn a tidy little profit. A house and a guest house right in the heart of Santa Fe seemed an appealing idea. Other such properties that I had seen always had a big price tag, and seemed to sell well. So I called Sidi and told him my idea. Now, my nafs wanted these houses. I had already committed to buy one of them, and had closed on it, but the second was still in escrow. I had spent quite a bit of time imagining how great this was going to be, and how much money I was going to make.

There were many reasons I wanted to remodel these houses. One was that I love beauty, and enjoy creating great spaces. Art has always been an important part of my life. It is said that art is a step from nature toward the infinite. I do believe that the greatest art is the art we make of our lives but, nonetheless, I have always appreciated and been inspired by beautiful things. A hadith says, **"Allah is beautiful and Allah loves beauty."** Sidi says in *Music of the Soul,* "The cause of love is beauty, for Allah's love spreads to all creation and to everything in it, without restriction, because it is essentially beautiful, because it is the real existence of each thing, and He is beautiful."

Instead of just repainting and doing a bit of remodeling, I ended up gutting the first house and creating something that I needed to sell for quite a lot in order to get my money back. I put in beautiful hand-carved wooden skylights from Morocco; all the bathrooms had hand-painted sink cabinets from India and Morocco; the kitchen had hand-painted cabinets, and 100 year-old pantry doors from Morocco.

I thought when I had finished this project, I would have enough capital from the sale of this mini-estate to buy and fix up some more properties. I was seeing myself as the Donald Trump of Santa Fe. So when I brought up the subject of these two houses with Sidi, I was careful how I spoke about them. There was no part of me that wanted to hear even a suggestion of "Salih, that is a terrible idea." I wanted to hear that it was quite smart, and that I would reap great financial rewards.

Here is how I brought it all up: "Sidi, I just bought a couple of houses side by side in Santa Fe, which share a yard. I got great prices on these houses. I want to fix them up, join them together as one property, and sell them as a main house and guest house. Can I have your blessing on this project?" He responded:

Bismillah. (Meaning..."in the name of God")

Now this was exactly the response my nafs wanted to hear. After I got this response, I said: "So Sidi, do you see that this will all work out alright?"

Trust Allah.

I was asking questions in a way that might get the answers I wanted. So I bought both houses, sunk a ton of money into remodeling, got them to a point where they were too overpriced for the neighborhood, had a tough time selling them, got into more debt than I could handle, created great stress for myself, and thus and put myself into a big fire.

I was trying to sell the compound for almost a million dollars, and had no offers at all. Some people showed interest, but a sale never manifested. Then I got an offer for the smaller of the two houses, and decided to sell it, because carrying the two mortgages was too much for me. The offer was a lot less than I wanted, so I called Sidi and asked if I should accept the offer.

Enough for you. Sell the house.

Later, while traveling with Sidi, I asked him why I was having so much trouble selling the bigger house. I was living next door in a rented house, and it was not nearly as nice as the one I had remodeled. However, I had rented out the big house for $400 a month more than I was paying for the house I was in, so I thought the extra $4800 a year was worth it. Also, I didn't want to move into the house, only to have it sell. I had been fortunate to find a rental just next door to the houses I was remodeling, which made it much easier to check up on things.

So when I asked Sidi what the problem was, he told me that the location was still not right for the price I was asking. I knew he had known this all along. But when I originally asked the question, I didn't ask him if it was a good idea, if the house was in the right location, if the price was right...no part of the question opened the door to the response that I should not do it, or that I should buy them, but not put so much into them. He went on to add that I got a tremendous amount of education from this experience, and that what I had gained and learned would far outweigh any consequences. **He has taught me two important things: We learn from our mistakes, and we grow from our misfortunes.**

My experience with Sidi has been that he often allows us just enough rope to have a learning experience without hanging ourselves. And he won't give responses that we are either unwilling or unready to hear and assimilate.

During my first stay in Jerusalem, I asked Sidi repeatedly if Nathalie, my wife, would come back to me. *Would she stay with me? Would my marriage stay together? Would my family stay intact?* I think he always knew that we would not stay married in the end, but he also knew I wasn't ready to hear that. So he gave me what my heart needed and could contain at the moment—which was that she would return and things would work out. It isn't that he didn't tell me the truth; rather, he said it in words that left room for me to hear what I needed to hear. She did return for a while, and then left again. But things did work out in the sense that, even though we're divorced, I am once again truly and authentically happy. For that I always thank Sidi, may Allah bless him and keep him always. He told me true love can never have a divorce, because in true love, Allah is the lover and the loved, and I believe this to be true.

Eventually, the man who had been renting the larger house left because he bought a home, and I was both happy and sad to see him go. He told me before moving in that he had nice furniture and the house would look elegant. In reality, it was messy and looked pretty awful while he lived there so, when the realtor showed it, people didn't see the value. The realtor wanted me to ask the renter to leave, but I needed the money and was fearful I wouldn't find someone else. Plus I really liked him, and felt a lot of compassion for him because he was recently divorced and was alone with his two sons. When he did leave, I found no more renters. (People don't like renting houses that are being shown, especially when the rent is expensive.) So instead, I moved into the house myself.

I fell in love with it the first night, and called the next morning to take it off the market. And as I write this I am elated to be living here.

I know in my heart that Sidi saw all of this before it happened. I think he always saw that I would one day live in the house. At the time I originally called him about it, my financial position was quite weak, as I was just starting to build a new business and had little income. At this point, I was divorced and living on my own with my youngest daughter, and cash flow was pretty disastrous. The divorce was financially devastating, and I am still coming to terms with it. Yet I am sure Sidi saw that things would improve, and I would be alright. Thus, when he said, "Trust Allah," he knew exactly what the outcome would be.

I try to be careful of asking too many questions concerned with the dunya (material world). I want to use what he has taught me to figure things out for myself. So when a question arises, I ask myself, *What would Sidi answer?* I think I've gotten pretty clear on what he would say most of the time.

I had a friend a while ago, who has since passed away, but who always seemed to be in a good mood, no matter how challenging his circumstances were. I once asked him how he dealt with all these challenges, and yet seemed to always be smiling. His response was, "I just think of what Fred Astaire would have done in the same situation." So now I think, "What would Sidi do in this situation?"

Many things in my life were interwoven around these houses, and there were many valuable lessons to be learned. When I originally mentioned them to Sidi, I think he knew in advance that I was going to go through these experiences. If I had authentically wanted to know about everything in advance, I could have asked my questions much more precisely. I could have said things like, *Will these houses make me money? Is this a good investment? Is this what I should be doing? Would it be better to not buy these houses? Should I be doing something else?*

But I didn't ask these questions because my nafs wanted in, and my personality didn't want to hear no. As I look back on all this, it seems that maybe Allah placed a veil over anyone who considered buying the house in which I now live, so that it would be kept available for me. All my visitors say that this house is a good reflection of me, so I guess there are some destinies we are meant to live out.

Each time I would bring up the issue of the houses, and why they weren't selling, Sidi would tell me to "be patient" and "trust Allah." **In fact, "be patient" and "trust Allah" appear to be two simple commands, but they can have a total and profound effect on one's life.**

The Pure White Mind

I could feel the cold penetrate my heart and body as I greeted the early morning in Jerusalem. Having slept poorly—because the night was still daytime for my body, because my mind was in such a state of confusion, because my heart was in such a state of unrest—I felt the tiredness profoundly. Lack of sleep was probably good for me because my spiritually and emotionally vulnerable state left no identifiable defense system to count on. Though I know now it wasn't true, I felt I was open to letting go of all my preconceived ideas, or "pictures," as Sidi would call them.

For instance, I believed that I could identify my pain and its origins, but I was at a loss to find a remedy or a cure for that pain and was counting on Sidi to help me with this. **I suppose my innermost self knew that surrendering to Allah was the answer; but consciously, I was far from able to assimilate such information—and even further from being able to accomplish such a thing.**

I've learned that one of the ways we learn to surrender to Allah is to first surrender to the guide. But having never had a real guide, or never having within me the vision to recognize a real guide, I had always forged my own path. As a result of following the ideas of Christian mystics; studying the ways of the Torah and Kabala; getting involved in Hinduism, Buddhism and a lot of other "isms"; and meeting and reading the concepts of other Sufis, my inner knowledge consisted of a hodge-podge of philosophies. There were no real, cohesive practices with which to build a container to hold authentic enlightenment.

I certainly considered myself quite advanced along the spiritual path—but all it took was one strong shot of fire, and I was reduced to a bumbling idiot. It was easy to love Allah and stand strong in the garden, but when I got a taste of the fire, I was quickly humbled. (In writing this thought, I almost stated *when Allah put me in the fire*—actually, I put myself in the fire with my pride, arrogance and know-it-all attitude.) I used to say *Allah did this* and *Allah did that;* now I realize that Allah allows a lot of things to happen, but this does not necessarily mean it is His desire. I would sometimes wonder why Allah sent me temptations and trials; today I realize that I am the one who creates these things. If anyone sends temptations, it is not Allah; it is the Shaitan. The Shaitan is Iblis, the Devil, the angel who did not bow down to Adam. Allah allows these temptations for a good reason.

As I mentioned, one of the teachings I chose to read my first morning in Jerusalem was *Adam, The Caliph of Allah,* the story of our origins. Allah placed Iblis at the door to the garden of His presence so that we would be sure to have our hearts cleaned of all impurities when we find ourselves in this exalted state. Iblis sends us temptations for our own good, and our own cleaning. He helps us recognize our improper desires, and allows us to cleanse and purify our being, so that we do not bring dirty water to the sacred garden.

Thus, when we are not clean, when all our nafs are not purified, we cannot enter the garden. If our hearts and being are full of love, truth and light, this will overcome the temptations of Iblis, and we will be accepted into the garden.

I cannot tell you how many times I have been ashamed of who I am in front of my guide. Even when I am not physically before him, distance has no impact on his sight. When I made my first trip to Sidi in Jerusalem, it was fortunate that I didn't know the depth of his seeing. Otherwise, I would have been too embarrassed to show up. **Being with Sidi is good practice for those of us who want to be able to resist Iblis. The mirror Sidi holds up to us enables us to see ourselves more clearly, and start the inner work we must do to cleanse ourselves. We come from a divine source that creates perfection. By treasuring ourselves and others we treasure the divine love from which we come.**

Later in my trip, Nathalie called Sidi's house to tell me she had finished her visit with her boyfriend, and was heading back to Santa Fe. I was not staying in the house, but below in the zawiyah, so I did not talk to her. But he did. I asked him what he heard in her voice. He said, "She comes from the deep polite." In Sufi terms, "the polite" is the adab, which refers to right conduct and impeccable manners. This is not innate within my being, yet it is for Nathalie. She knows a lot about certain kinds of politeness and, fortunately, she has educated our children with this knowledge. But I am always concerned with my adab in front of Sidi, and have a lot of fear around my level of adab with Allah. **Holding the adab with all of creation is one way we can hold the adab with Allah. Sidi says, "Allah sees the black ant on the black rock on the moonless night." So I know that I can hide nothing from either of them. The more I experience the depth of Sidi's seeing, the more concerned I become. Yet I am also the more grateful for this awakening (that Allah sees all).**

My heart was alive and singing as I read through *Adam, The Caliph of Allah.* I started to understand how Allah created us in order to witness Himself, how He placed His qualities in us in order to experience Himself. He hid Himself deep within us so that we would have to remove the veils to drink from His cup. Sidi likened this to wearing 99 different layers of clothing, with every piece having two sides. The clothing can protect you from the cold, but you must remove each layer in order to have real warmth, which is only found in the comfort of the divine presence.

Adam was the first prophet, the bringer of news from the unseen, and he contains all the positive qualities that exist. Our own individual humanity will remain a secret to us until we can understand the meaning of the Adamic form. The story of Adam reveals many of these meanings. The birth of Adam was also a spiritual event; we must experience it internally in order to constantly renew ourselves. We were created for this purpose, to give birth to spiritual realizations. Yet these realizations will depend on our state of receptivity, which can be greatly enhanced by following a guide such as Sidi. Adam represents all the possibilities inherent within ourselves because, from Allah, Adam gave birth to his own wife. And through them came all of human creation. With Eve, Adam was able to establish love and multiply. Their act of creation, of sexual union, represents the possibilities of our own union with the divine. The principle of birth from the union of Adam and Eve, from the union of man and woman, culminates in the appearance of mankind and is, I believe, the most evident symbol of God.

The flow of Sidi's teachings kept getting interrupted by my dark mind. I found myself imagining my wife in the arms of another man, finding pleasure in his touch. I beat myself up mentally, emotionally and spiritually, and castrated myself with thoughts of impotence in relation to another man. No tears were enough to erase the pain, and I couldn't sustain enough concentration to turn from all the negativity. I worried about my children and how I would take care of them. I wondered how it would affect them to see me emasculated and depressed. This wasn't Iblis at the door to the garden; I was a million miles from the door to any garden, and my nafs was having a field day. One dark thought led to another, and each one fed a hundred others. This was not the garden of light; it was manure spread on the garden of darkness, composting and nurturing my negative thoughts. I am sure Iblis was dancing in circles of joy over my distress.

Maryam must have heard my crying, because she came again into the room and held me. I can't remember now what she said, or even if she said anything. She just knew my pain, and knew that I had to go through it. **I had to allow myself to**

disintegrate completely, and trust that Sidi would hold my heart together.

At that time I blamed almost everything wrong in my life on my wife. Yet I want to make it clear that this was because I was unwilling to accept my role in driving her away, and wanted to deny responsibility for my part in creating these circumstances. As you read this, please do not judge her, or anyone, in the way I did. As I grew more and learned to accept my role in our separation, I came to see her in a completely different light. This is part of my healing that I will share with you.

Sidi knew at exactly what time of my life I would be able to perceive things differently. And even though it took years, I feel I have arrived in a much more compassionate place. Through his guidance and teaching, I was able to gradually open my heart again. So the statements I make about Nathalie in the context of this story refer to feelings I had then. They were not necessarily truth, but I feel it is important to share them, though I am in no way proud to have had them. I have asked much forgiveness from Allah for the way I spoke about her in front of my children and others. If a human can excuse you, what of the one who created you?

I was seeing Nathalie through the eye of my nafs, not through the eye of my Lord. Sidi teaches us to see with Allah's eyes and hear with his ears, especially if you want to see Him. **When we look with the eye of the body, we see only a human being when we look at Sidi. But when we** look through the eye of our heart, we see the essence of the prophets, which is what he revealed to me that first night in the zawiyah. If we want to see and experience the essence of another, if we truly wish to honor another, we must look from within the deepest part of our being. When we learn to see with the light and love of Allah, we pierce the veils of our gross manifestations, and can see the subtlety of divine manifestation.

When Sidi reveals parts of himself that carry the light of the prophets, it is to show us our own potential. The prophets are examples of our own spiritual potential; to follow in their footsteps is to make a reality of this possibility. Sidi has total compassion, and all that he sees and hears and speaks comes from a place of beauty. We will do well to emulate this whenever possible.

Allah has 99 names, and these names reflect some of His qualities. Each of these qualities is a station we must walk through. But without Allah's grace and the help of a guide, it is impossible. It is from Allah's desire to know Himself that we are drawn to this knowing, and it is His love that draws us to Him. As Sidi says, "If He did not love you, you wouldn't hear Him calling to you now."

The guide can help us walk from the world of the gross to the essence of the soul, and I feel truly blessed by his presence in my life. Sidi has told me time and time again to use the name of Allah, to repeat it over and over again, to travel through all the qualities of Allah. If I want to see, I must know who is truly seeing, and if I want to hear, I must know who actually hears. In this manner, we can return to the essence, the origin, of these qualities as we experience them.

I was experiencing tremendous separation as I looked at Nathalie, and was far from feeling the unity that is the basis of Sidi's teachings. We were two separate entities and, though I felt entwined with her, I saw and experienced her as being far from me. When Adam looked upon Eve, he saw himself, not another. When I looked upon my wife, I saw someone totally different from me. I was looking with my nafs, not with my heart. I was seeing with my human eye, not my deep eye. My love was blocked; my heart was shut down.

The sounds of the morning call to prayer brought me back to my present situation. At that time I was not praying regularly. In fact, I didn't know the prayers. I had studied and read about Islam, about Islamic Sufism in particular, but I had no knowledge of the practices. My Sufi friend from Morocco was not at all like Sidi; though he taught me a lot about life and Sufism, he did not teach me about orthodox Islam. He taught mostly through stories.

Maryam came in and asked if I wanted to pray, so I followed her movements. She was incredibly patient with me during those first days as I struggled to learn the prayers. I was inspired by the depth of her commitment and her willingness to accept the rigors of her life there. She was a fountain of knowledge, who shared willingly—and it was a blessing to have someone to help me. The fact that she came to Sidi from outside Islam was useful for me, because she understood my struggles with learning the prayers and understanding the culture.

In those days Maryam lived simply. This helped her build an inner strength and a strong resilience to the elements. She knew how to deal with hardship, both physical and spiritual, and the discipline with which she lived her life on a daily basis enabled her to accomplish much. The stack of papers That sat at my bedside reflected untold hours of dedication.

There were others involved, of course. But for years and years, Maryam managed to keep in place all that had been done, as well as do a lot more herself. She would take the bus to her teaching job at the university, do all the shopping, cook for others when they came to the zawiyah, and generally take care of many broken-hearted seekers such as myself. She had come to Sidi from a farm in France so she knew about hard work and caring for animals; she helped take care of whatever animals were around the zawiyah, including the wounded animal that I was.

For many years I corresponded by mail with Maryam, and her letters were always full of the love of Allah. When beloveds wrote to Sidi, it was usually her hand that crafted the response. This was before the days of e-mail, and before people got in the habit of calling on the phone.

There were benefits to this type of learning and correspondence, because a question sat in the heart and "cooked" longer. When beloveds wanted to ask a question, they would form it in a letter and send it off to Jerusalem. It could be weeks before an answer would come back. This gave seekers a lot more time to reflect on what their hearts told them; often, they found their answers within themselves, as Sidi sent his spirit to them. A lot of these questions, along with Sidi's responses, formed the content of Sidi's first book published in the United States, called *Fruits From the Tree of Life*, published back in 1995.

I read many of these questions during those days in Jerusalem. **I realized that many hearts sought the same answers I was seeking, so when Sidi answered their questions, he was answering mine as well. We are all one heart, one mind, one body and one spirit.** When no separation exists between us, everything is shared. The pain I felt then was not just my pain. It was the pain of my children, the pain in the heart of my wife, the pain in the heart of everyone who was feeling lost and broken-hearted. I just wasn't aware of how many people suffered from the pain of broken love until I experienced it myself.

Humans possess something called a "reticular activating system," which works as a kind of filter: When you feel something is important in your life, information relevant to the thing you feel to be important is allowed through this filter. When a couple gets ready to have a baby, it seems everyone they meet is going through the same thing; when you are interested in pregnant women, you will notice them, whereas someone else might pass ten pregnant women without a second thought. When you buy a certain car, you start to see that car all over the place. When you have a bulldog, and love bulldogs, you will notice them all the time, whereas others will not give them any consideration.

I love seeking to know Allah, so I am aware when I run into others seeking the same thing. I love helping people who want to work from home, creating predictable, sustainable long-term income—so I notice people who talk of hating their job, looking for work, or wanting to start their own business. Because I love tennis, I will be aware of who is winning a certain match, while you might not have heard of the players because you have no interest in tennis.

When I took photos, all my energy and focus was narrowed down to a small, isolated area visible through the viewing hole. I was so focused on what was happening in that hole, so aware of what was happening in the focused area of my intent, that I was oblivious to what was going on around me. I was filtering out things that were not relevant to me. Yet I could sense the movement of the sun; I could feel anything in the surrounding area that might improve the photo I was building; I was aware of subtle shifts of light and the movement of the clouds, though I couldn't see them in the small viewing area.

Our reticular activating system filters out a lot of unnecessary information so that our minds do not overload. It protects us from an already existing assault on our senses. Sidi knows how to work with this to help us focus on things that are valuable to us. He opens our awareness, and guides us to see and hear things that we might have missed before. This is one of the ways our veils can be lifted. Through an intense focus of energy, we can penetrate into deeper layers of seeing, and gain understanding that might otherwise escape us.

As Sidi teaches, the value of the practices is that they strengthen us, so we can stand strong in the face of the storm and continue to examine our situation. The spiritual sense of a person is evident in the way they deal with adversity. It isn't hard to stand strong while all is going well, but we are truly tested when we have to make decisions in times of adversity. The following story is told in much detail, because I want to emphasize how many times during the hour in which this experience took place I was given opportunities to make choices that could have affected the rest of my family's life and mine.

Many years ago, when I was a photographer living in Paris, I had an experience that tested me, and helped me find out who I was. It was before I met Sidi; I was living a dunya (material) life, and wasn't too involved with concerns of the spirit. I was married at the time. One afternoon, I stopped to visit a girl who had been modeling for me, and now wanted to start a career in hair and make-up. She had asked me to look at her portfolio. At the time, I was smoking quite a bit of hash. When I got to her house, she asked if I had anything to smoke. I said I did, and gave her some hash in a little pipe I carried with me.

What happened next was truly frightening. Suddenly, she
started "freaking out," and became hysterical. She became
unbelievably paranoid, and accused me of putting
"something special" in the hash so I could sleep with her.
Then she went rigid and began gasping for air; she said she
couldn't breathe. At that point, I started to panic, and didn't
know what to do. So I immediately picked up the phone and
called the operator, asking for the equivalent of our 911 for
emergencies. She transferred me to a number for the police;
when they answered, I quickly stated that someone was in
distress and they needed to send an ambulance.

The lady on the phone put me on hold, saying she would
connect me with the right people. I waited for what seemed
like an eternity. Remember, this girl was screaming, and I was
frightened that something was terribly wrong and she might
die. I wondered: *If she dies, what will happen to me? Will I go to
prison?*

After a few minutes of waiting, I hung up and dialed the
operator again. I said I needed help immediately, but the
police had put me on hold. She suggested the fire
department, and connected me. I repeated the story, telling
them exactly what happened, and they said they could be
there in a matter of minutes with first aid. I gave them the
address, the apartment number and phone number, and
asked them what to do in the meantime. They said to ask her
if she had any medication that would calm her down, and to
keep talking with her and walk her around so she wouldn't
black out.

I hung up the phone and went back to her. I told her I had called for help and asked if she had any medication that would calm her down. She screamed that she was dying, and that I had done it to her, and to leave her alone. At that point, my dark mind came on strong, and I questioned whether I should even stay there. I felt sure that, no matter what happened to her, I would be arrested and sent to jail for possession of drugs—at the least. A huge part of me said I had done all I could, that help was on the way, and the best and smartest thing to do was to get out before the authorities showed up. (I was pretty well-known in Paris at the time as a photographer. I worked for most of the top magazines, and hung out with many known personalities and rock groups, the most famous of which was the Rolling Stones. More than once, we had experienced conflicts with the police over drugs, so I felt they would be happy to put me away.) I couldn't even get my mind around what would happen if the girl died.

The girl's condition continued to deteriorate. I hauled her to her feet and walked her out toward the balcony. She started to pull back, as if she thought I was going to throw her over the railing. Her paranoia was accentuated, and I was growing increasingly dysfunctional myself.

Sidi says in his teaching *The Man With the Pure White Mind is a Perfect Holy World,* that we must go through all the outward experiences and act righteously. In fact, one of the qualities of the name he gave me—Salih—is righteousness. **As God appears in everything in a divine way, and gives unto each** thing its own qualities, its own fragrance, it thus becomes an expression of divine revelation. Allah wants us filled with these graces; He wants our hearts to be full of His love because this proves His presence. So when we receive an order, and we comply with it, we come to understand it more, in a deeper and more profound way. Sidi guides us to open our hearts, and know the proper way to be, the adab. The closer we are to God, the more we are held accountable for our actions.

We are taught that Allah sees the intent in our hearts, and this intent carries the most weight. If we hurt someone intentionally, it isn't the same as hurting someone unintentionally. If I swerve to avoid hitting someone, and still cause injury to another, it isn't the same as if I deliberately run over someone. God wants us to absorb and take into our beings the true quality of every manifestation. When we develop these manifestations of existence within us, we develop ourselves, and we thus fulfill God's purpose of knowing Himself through us.

So we should strive to have the divine qualities shine through us, whether in the most ordinary or challenging of situations. I would like the qualities of love, truth, mercy and compassion (to name just a few) to always be present and flowing through me, no matter what happens.

Our view of the world reflects our level of self-respect. When we trust ourselves, we are really trusting the divine love that created us, and when we fail to honor ourselves, we are in denial of that divinity—as Sidi teaches, God does not create things He has no love for. And when we don't respect ourselves, it is more challenging to respect others, as we can't give what we don't have. To heal pain in ourselves, or help others to heal, we should focus on light and love, and look for that which is valuable and meaningful. We should not focus on that which carries lesser value and worth, because the good things have more connection to divine love.

Resistance grows from thoughts that come from our mind rather than our divine connection. Accepting and understanding, with appreciation, allows us to feel better and more connected. When you deny yourself approval, how can you offer it to others? This was to be one of the major changes I would go through, as Sidi told me regularly, "Allah loves you more than you love yourself."

But the dark mind and the shaitan fight for our attention, and when we are weakened they quickly attack our weaknesses. That day in the girl's apartment, I was particularly vulnerable to the dark mind, because I was in love with the dunya and not focused on strengthening my spirit. **Obedience to the divine spirit brings peace and contentment to one's being, while following the nafs eventually will lead to a stressful and conflicted state of being.** When you trust righteousness and follow the orders—when you realize their power—your entire being not only accepts them willingly, but does so in gratitude, with a heart full of praise for the chance you have to be in this level of awareness. Babies are mostly happy and content because they do not judge themselves or compare themselves to others. They are thus more connected to their source energy.

Sidi teaches us that we are not obedient to other people, but to God Himself. When we are in a relationship with another beloved, we love Allah through the face of the person we love. So if we seemingly act in obedience to an order from this person, we are in reality obeying God.

At that time in Paris, I was not at a level of awareness to see such truths. What I saw was that, if I stuck around in that apartment, I could end up in jail. It could ruin my life and negatively affect the lives of my family. I saw nothing positive about sticking around. I knew competent help was on the way. I felt I had done everything I could. Yet there was, and I thank Allah, a part of me that fought these dark thoughts. A part of me realized I couldn't leave her alone. And as she was in an apartment, on a high floor, there was no way I could get down the single elevator without being seen.

If I waited until the fire department arrived, they would see me leave. I wondered if there were stairs, so that I could walk down when I saw them come out of the elevator. Then I wondered what would happen if she lived and later told them my name. How would I explain why I left?

There are quite a few moments that define our lives. This was a defining moment for me, and somewhere a part of me knew it. If I left, I would never be able to undo it. In my life today, I don't think there would even be a battle. I would not consider running away. But back then, I had to find reasons to stay. And I simply wasn't coming up with any that made better sense than to run. Plus, I was running out of time, because the fire department was on the way.

It took much longer than I thought, so I tried the police again. Again I couldn't get through. So I called the fire department back, and asked where they were. *Three, four minutes away,* I was told. My breath was getting short. The girl was almost rigid and, though she had stopped screaming, I could feel her hands and face getting cold. In turn, I was frozen in fear.

My contentment with myself at that time of my life was more about an image of spirituality I put forth than an actual commitment to a rigorous path of truth. I practiced a false obedience, because it was more about what would impress others than about pleasing God. I was facing a moment of truth. Who was I? What was I made of?

The White Mind teaching warns us about barren obedience and straying from pure morals. **The desire to impress others is what Sidi calls a "mischief"; he advises us to run away from them and turn to God.** In that Paris apartment, what I wanted to run away from was the situation. I had no conscious awareness of the presence of God, even though I know now that God was present.

Carl Jung was once asked if he thought there was a God. "I don't think there is a God," he said. "I know there is a God." I did not have that certainty. I once asked a yogi friend how he would define God. "G-O-D," he said. "G is for Guide, O is for of, D is for destiny—so God means guide of destiny." God was indeed guiding my destiny that day in Paris. I wanted so badly to get out of there, but something in my conscience would not allow it.

In *The White Mind*, Sidi teaches that what we see in another is a reflection of a part of ourselves. For instance: If we have a reaction to greed in someone else, it is a reflection of our own unresolved issues with greed. I think we all have aspects of ourselves that look at other aspects of ourselves, just the way we look at each other: Just as we might judge another, one part of ourselves judges other parts of ourselves. We seek unity not only with others, but within ourselves, for all the unresolved issues we carry around.

We have to live with the choices we make in our lives, and the quality of our lives is determined by the quality of our choices. I knew I was at a turning point. I don't think I had much of a conscience as I grew up. If I told a lie—and I told plenty of them—I didn't consciously suffer any guilty feelings. I used to make up all kinds of things to impress or manipulate people. I have stolen from people; I have damaged things and not been honest about my part in what happened; I have hurt people through my actions.

Fortunately we are taught on this path how to ask forgiveness and make repentance, how to wipe the slate clean. Sidi teaches us that Allah does not punish those He loves for their sins; He gives them a chance to say they are sorry and ask forgiveness. But at the moment of which I write, I was caught in a deep and tangled web of my own making. Even though it was a little late, and I wasn't what one would call a real believer, I did beg God to help me get out of the situation. I promised all kinds of things if He would help. It wasn't the first time I had turned to God in desperation, and there were other times later, when I found myself doing the same thing. While I wrestled with all of this, a lot of my focus and attention was still on the girl, making her talk and trying to stop her from becoming completely catatonic.

I had opened the door to the apartment. Finally, I heard the elevator door open. I rushed out to see the firemen arriving. One of them came to me and asked me to tell him everything that had happened. I told him the complete truth: She had smoked a few puffs of strong hash, and it had immediately affected her negatively. He asked if I hadn't given her something else, and I promised I hadn't. He asked if she had been drinking, and I said I didn't think so. The others were trying to talk to her, but she was non-responsive. I saw them give her a shot with a syringe.

The first man continued to interrogate me: *Where I had gotten the hash? How much did I have with me? Was I trying to sell it?* I was getting more and more nervous. The girl seemed to respond to the shot, and her muscles relaxed. She began to be a bit coherent, and told them that I had drugged her with something that affected her badly. She also mentioned she had a blood sugar problem.

The next thing I remember is them putting her on a stretcher. They said they were taking her to a hospital, and I had to come along. In the elevator on the way down, I asked if she would be alright. I was assured she was out of danger, but they had to take her to the hospital for surveillance. When we got outside and they put her in the ambulance, I asked the man what I was to do. He asked how I had gotten there; I responded that I was on my motorcycle. He then told me to get my motorcycle and follow the ambulance to the hospital. He would meet me there. I walked away, relieved that she would be alright, and nervous about what would happen next. On the way to the hospital, I realized they still hadn't even asked my name…If I just drifted a bit further back, I could easily take a turn and disappear. But though I was strongly tempted, I continued on to the hospital.

When I got there, the fireman who had interviewed me pulled me aside and continued to interrogate me about the hash. I had told him repeatedly that it was a strong hash—the best I had ever seen—and maybe the girl wasn't accustomed to such good stuff. I told him again that I had called the police twice but had never gotten through. He said I was lucky because, if I had gotten through to the police, I would be on my way to jail. It thus became apparent to me that God was looking out for me in this whole situation. I believe to this day that there was more than luck involved, in that the police never answered the call. And then, to my utter astonishment, the fireman pulled me further aside and whispered: "Can you spare some of that hash, so I could have some?"

To this day, I don't think I've repeated this story to more than one or two people. It might seem a bit out of place in this narrative, but it appeared in my thoughts as I was writing. And in sharing what happened, I have learned a lot that I hadn't thought about before: I believe Allah was present, and looking out for me. I wonder how my life would have changed if I had run away. Maybe I earned some "brownie points" by standing my ground. I am certainly not proud of the whole incident. I never told my wife about it; she would have wondered why I was smoking hash in the middle of the afternoon in some girl's apartment. I know that, if I'm honest with myself, I probably didn't have the cleanest of intentions. But I have changed a lot since that time, and hardly recognize who I was back then.

It was like a lifetime was condensed into a few minutes during that incident, and those minutes are a microcosm of that period of my life.

In *The White Mind*, Sidi says that our shortcomings prevent the light from reaching us, because they prevent us from following the pure mind. When we stop following the highest way, we are distracted and more vulnerable to the temptations of the shaitan. It is important to follow the way without pride or arrogance.

Just as we have material nafs, we are also tempted by spiritual nafs, such as the desire to be holier or more spiritual than someone else. **When we look at others in a way that makes them less than ourselves, we only show our own** weakness. **With this act of judgment, we separate ourselves from the heart of a brother or sister. When we diminish another in order to elevate ourselves, we create a space between us. And this space creates a nice landing spot and home for the shaitan.**

In *The White Mind*, Sidi explores the great gift a person gives through disobedience to the divine order. In contrast to what you witness, you also get to experience the majesty of the divine order. When you see someone falling into darkness and sin, you experience the baser nature of material nafs, and the nature of sin. This increases one's desire to stay with Allah, rather than find yourself in similar circumstances. I can only pray that my life of sin may have shown others what a wasted life it was, and helped them turn toward the light.

It is said that if we didn't sin, Allah would create someone else who did, because He is the forgiver and, without sin, we rob Him of the quality of forgiveness. If you are still in a state where you knowingly sin, then look at those who don't and ask Allah's blessings to be showered upon them, because they are awakening you from your own weakened state. **The sins of others are but a mirror in which we can see parts of our own nature reflected. If you consider any person as less than yourself, you are diminishing yourself by not following the pure white mind.**

The Secret of the Love of God

I know that the universe is full of magical moments, just waiting for us to open our hearts so that we can experience them. But with my heart closed, I greeted each new day with a heavy heart, and couldn't feel the magic. I cannot even imagine what the world must look like through Sidi's eyes, because he sees with the eye of Allah, not just the eye of humanity. I have thought that, if I could somehow get a bird's-eye view of my life, I would see myself surrounded by hundreds of opportunities and possibilities that I cannot see from the prison in which I currently reside.

On that first visit to Jerusalem, I did feel that the teachings by my bed held a key to unlock the door of at least one room of this prison. When in prison, you may think that, if you can just escape from the room you are in, you will be free—but there is always the chance that one locked room will only lead to another, so it's hard to know just how many doors you might have to go through. I desperately wanted to fly again, to feel the freedom I believed I had felt before Nathalie left. I had felt so happy before, and still had no idea how much of that happiness was illusory. **I didn't know I was actually in a prison all that time, confined by the limitations of my spiritual awareness.**

Comfort can be a huge trap, and the sad thing is that, for all those years, I had no conscious idea of the illusory nature of my existence. I was comfortable most of the time. I had a great family and a beautiful wife; I traveled the world taking photos I thought were pretty good; I lived in a big, spacious house; I had reached what I and many others thought of as the American dream. But I had also learned that whatever happiness I felt was sourced from and dependent upon things that were outside myself, rather than inner substance. In *The Secret of the Love of God*, Sidi writes about the real love, the love that leads you to the heart of the real Beloved, the love that frees you from limitation because of the limitless nature of the real Beloved. Sidi writes: "As Allah says to His prophet David, *I forbid the hearts of My lovers any love except My love.*"

Love for the material world and material things is not the same as love for Allah. If we are not careful, it can separate us from the actual thing we seek, the very purpose of our existence, which I believe to be unity with God. Islam teaches us to love Allah as if we see Allah, and know that even if we don't see Him, He sees us. When we love people, one should see Allah in them. I felt that I loved my wife but, if that love had been the real love of which Sidi speaks, it would not have been dependent upon her loving me back.

When I was with the girl in the apartment, I was not aware of loving Allah. But as I went back over that incident in my mind, so that I could share the story with you, I realized that God loved me through those moments. I was being taught something of great importance, but I believe I was also being protected and guided with love.

In *The Secret of the Love of God,* Sidi explains what happens
when we love someone the way I loved my wife. When we
don't fully grasp what moves us to love a person—when we
love someone, but stop with the outside picture—then we
only touch some of the love, rather than the total fullness of
the love that moves us. In fact, the outside picture to which
we are attached is a veil between us and this essence.

I will be forever grateful for the time I shared with my wife. I
can now accept responsibility for much of what happened. If
I had understood more about the real love, she might have
felt differently, and more fulfilled in the experience of her
relationship with me. I know that the love of my children
was, and is, more unconditional than the love I shared with
her. **This is because I do experience and see the heart of
Allah in my children, and I love more than the outside picture. I love their essence, their souls, the origin of who they
are. Our bodies disappear in this love, leaving my essence
to love their essence. And this is how a man should love a
woman. Because when this happens, all the veils disappear
in the unity that is experienced; the bodies disappear, and it
is God loving Himself, not a person loving a person.**

Though translations may make the words differ, it is written
in a Hadith Qudsi that Allah said, "I was a hidden treasure
desiring to be known, so I manifested all of creation to reveal
the essence of the deep, secret knowing of myself. He whom I
created to reveal the treasure carries within himself this
treasure, but he must explode the mountain of his existence
to discover the treasure which is hidden within it."

Even though I read these words that day in Jerusalem, I can't honestly say I understood their meaning. With these words, Sidi planted seeds in my heart, and he watered these seeds for years with the flow of love, compassion, mercy, patience and other attributes that he showered on my heart. **"You can't eat the apple in one bite," he would say. "Be patient and trust Allah."** You have no idea what patience he had with me and my incessant questions. He would tell me the same thing over and over, yet I never felt impatience in his words. As I understand his teaching on it, the essential reality of patience is that it prevents the soul from complaining, and it is an attribute of love.

When we love the outside picture of a person, we are not only veiled from this person, but from the rest of existence as well, because we do not truly understand the deep, secret meaning of the real love. The body of our existence is thus a veil as well. Sidi says it is "like a mountain in which the treasure is concealed, and Allah created this mountain of His water and clay, exactly in order that He could bury His treasure within it."

I read this numerous times without grasping the meaning. **There are so many layers under each word Sidi writes, and so many secrets hidden in each phrase, that his ideas can only be revealed one layer at a time.**

I can't remember exactly what I did for most of that day. I know Maryam explained that Sidi went to the mosque, where he had an office, and that I would see him when he returned

that evening. I think I went out with Maryam to get some
groceries, but most of the day I sat in the room, and read and
wrote the teachings. As I mentioned previously, at that time
none of Sidi's teachings were published in English; all I could
take from the zawiyah was what I could copy by hand. Just
reading was not enough—I had to write each word if I
wanted to ground myself in these teachings. (Even today,
with all the published books, Sidi teaches his beloveds to
write the teachings. Each new book should be hand-copied,
each word written by our own hand.)

I still have the teachings I copied in Jerusalem. Over the
years, I have continued to copy teachings—not only Sidi's,
but the Koran as well. One Ramadan I wrote by hand, in
Arabic, the entire surah of *The Cow*—all 286 verses. (The
Koran is composed of chapters, called surahs, and verses,
called ayats.) I wrote for hours every day, because writing in
Arabic took me a long time. I have written many other surahs
as well. Writing something by hand brings it deeper into your
heart, and I want to know this message in my heart. I want to
understand with more than my mind. I want to live these
teachings with every fiber of my being.

I have spent years trying to understand Arabic, because I
want to know this aspect of the Koran. First I had to learn the
alphabet, letter by letter. Then I had to put those letters
together, and know how the shapes of letters can change,
depending on where they are found in a word. Then I had to
understand the words the letters formed, and from there
learn all the different forms of the words (singular and plural

nouns, verb tenses). Then the words are strung together into sentences, and I have to learn the meaning, which is complicated because there can be many different translations of the subtler sentences. Then the sentences are linked together into an ayah, and the ayat are linked into surahs, etc.

For all the years I've been with Sidi, I'm still learning the meaning of the first surah of the Koran, called the Fatihah. Sometimes Sidi will draw one of the letters of the Fatihah, and reveal a meaning behind this letter that I have never experienced. He can then explain a single word, and reveal some of its secrets. He can share some of the secrets of the movements one makes during prayer. It is said that one can spend a lifetime praying five times a day, and not once perform a perfect salat (prayer).

It seems each year that goes by brings a deeper understanding of what is meant by this "mountain of existence," in which the secret is hidden. Sometimes I scream inside, because I feel so impotent and childlike in my inability to grasp the real meaning. **As each little veil is lifted, I see how many more there are. It's like coming out of a room of the prison, only to see that there are ten more—all with locked doors for which you must find the key. First you thought it was just one key...now you need ten.**

What keeps me going is that each room is more beautiful than the one I just left. And in some of the rooms, I even see light shining through a window. The first room, the one I was in when I first went to Sidi, was dark. I couldn't see any light;

there was no window and no view—just the deep, black darkness that my sister Nura held me in, and which my brother Tarik told me held the meaning of my existence. When I was in this place of darkness and emptiness, Tarik suggested that I should "fill the emptiness with love."

I had to leave this room and start a voyage, and there was no way I could speed up this voyage without guidance. I had spent my life rushing through experiences, always seeking the instant gratification of a result, and not sinking into the joyous experience of creation. I was going to have to learn patience if it killed me. And it probably would kill a part of me—a part of me that needed to go.

Sidi teaches that Allah's wisdom is behind everything and that the laws of Allah were written before creation. So behind the mountain of my existence, which prevented even a glimpse of what I sought, there was Allah's wisdom. And I had built a big mountain. Since that time, I have learned a lot about the material possessions I had accumulated. I thought that having a big house, lots of cars for the family, money in the bank, and work that produced a great income, would make me feel secure. I thought they were protection for my loved ones and me from any challenges we might face.

Sidi says we come into the world naked and we leave naked. None of these possessions can be taken with us. In the pain in which I found myself, these possessions were slowly becoming more of a hindrance than a help. In my depression, I was working less and less. The cost of maintaining my lifestyle was over five figures a month and, at that time, if I didn't work, I didn't earn money. So I was living on money I had put aside. A few hundred thousand dollars might seem like a lot of money, but it can disappear pretty fast when you have an overhead like the one I had.

Because my manhood was threatened at the time, as my wife turned her attention to another man, I was not ready to give up the material life that was, for me, another expression of my manhood. My nafs was being fed a pretty tasty meal with the outside picture of success that this lifestyle put forward. Yes, this was a pretty big mountain. I would have to do a lot of digging and destroying in order to find the secret that was hidden within.

Sidi was merciful in not showing me how big this mountain was, and how much work lay in front of me. I don't think I was strong enough at the time to face the journey that lay before me. I had to learn to destroy this mountain. I had to plant the seeds of a new yearning—for a different life, a different existence—in the core of this mountain. This yearning, which is called himma, had to be for God alone…not for a picture, or anything to do with the material world.

When this himma is truly authentic, it brings more and more himma, until the accumulated yearning finally explodes inside of you. Then the mountain starts to crumble, destroying veil upon veil, and revealing more and more of the secret. Then we learn to love another as Adam loved Eve, whom he knew to be of his own substance. When he entered her and penetrated her body, her body was a veil. But when he pierced the veil to touch her essence, he touched his own essence. He did not stop with the outside picture, as I had done with Nathalie. Adam used the fire of his himma to explode the mountain.

When the mountain disappears, a space appears—an opening to a new and deeper revelation. We start to experience things as less dense, and more full of light. The explosion of the accumulated himma creates a fire, which cleans and purifies our heart, so there can be still more himma and even more light. **As our heart fills with love, this love attracts more love (just as himma attracts more himma). The accumulated love starts to penetrate the barriers that have blocked its flow. As the dam breaks and the love starts flowing again, pain is washed away in the torrent of the river flowing toward the ocean of the real love—and we start to once again experience the sensation of the love that created us.**

Maybe Allah allows us the freedom to build our nafs so that, when we finally surrender to Him, we surrender something we thought held value. If someone gives a dollar from an accumulated wealth of a million dollars, does it have the same value as the gift of a child who gives all he has in his piggy bank? I always felt generous in my giving, but I realize now that I always gave what was easy to give. When I had to give up my attachments to the pictures I had about a wife and family, it became a whole different ball game. That had to be wrenched from me. But I believe we are never tested more than we can stand and that, with every test, there is support to withstand the rigors of that test.

One thing that was hard for me to grasp was how responsible I was for bringing on my test. As I said before, I don't think my situation was of Allah's creation. He allowed me the space to build that dense mountain of material existence, so one could say that, because everything comes from Allah, He was present in its creation. But this doesn't mean other factors weren't also present. The shaitan and my nafs had an awful lot to do with building my mountain. Allah, in His wisdom, allowed it to happen so that I could learn from it. He allowed me to build the illusion, knowing all along that, within my heart was the real love, the real himma— connected to and sourced from divine essence—with which I could destroy that mountain, penetrate some of the veils, and start the return to my original creation.

Allah, in His wisdom, sent Iblis to tempt me to clean my nafs, but to keep me from the real garden, because I was yet in an impure state. **One of the tools Sidi teaches us to help resist these temptations is that of adh-dhikr, or remembrance and repetition of the divine name, Allah. This remembrance keeps the space created open, and it continues to nourish us so that the heart stays open.**

I once learned an exercise in a seminar about cold-calling, one of the skills we are taught in my business. (Cold-calling requires telephoning people you don't know. Their names are on lists available for purchase; such lists consist of people that have expressed a specific interest, e.g., in a home-based business.) Making these calls can be challenging, because you hear "no" a lot. In this seminar, we were taught to raise your chin as high as you can, put the biggest grin on your face you can possibly muster, and force the grin as much as you can, until you are almost chuckling to yourself. If you try this, you'll see it feels so foolish that it's hard to be depressed or sad when you're doing it.

Unfortunately for me, remembrance was a lot more challenging, and it took a lot longer for my depression to lift, because it was a lot more subtle. When authentic, it comes from a deeper place and takes you to a deeper place. It was not for me an instant fix, which is what I was hoping for. I tell people, when sharing a health product with them, that you cannot undo 40 years of bad eating and lifestyle choices overnight. You can start by taking the first step and deciding to make different choices, but it will take a while to experience the benefits. You don't lose 50 pounds overnight, but making a choice to change, and then sticking with that choice, definitely has an accumulated benefit.

Sidi has taught me that no one state of being is necessarily better than another. We are not all the same, as Allah created diversity, and these differences allow us to experience variety, and it is this variety which creates an overall balance and harmony. Great diversity of beliefs also creates balance. Sidi has never really tried to change people's beliefs or encourage everyone to be the same. He is always accepting of people— he doesn't just tolerate them, he truly accepts them.

So the decisions to practice remembrance, to take Sidi's hand, and to immerse myself in Islam were choices that would have a long-term benefit in my life. But I had no idea how long it would take and I hoped, much more than I actually knew, that these decisions would work to my advantage.

In *The Secret of the Love of God*, Sidi writes that, once you start to eat of the fruits of these realizations, you are getting the real food. With this real food, you start to live the life you were created to live—and the nourishment that sustains this life is not what you thought nourished you before (i.e., material comfort). **The nourishment of this life is the fruit of the practices and the seeking that develops the himma. Once you've tasted this fruit, it's increasingly difficult to be satisfied by other food, which only satisfies hunger of a denser type, and does so for only a few moments at a time.** This food increases one's appetite, but increased amounts of this holy food do not make you fat and sick like the food of the material world. This food grows the internal fire that fuels your seeking to taste more of the real love. The growth in the intensity of my seeking, though it proved much slower than I would have liked, has built over the years to a point where things that had importance before are meaningless now, and my yearning is for things of a completely different nature.

He who loves Me, knows Me,
And he who knows Me, finds Me,
He who finds Me, becomes inflamed in My passion.
I have killed him so that I may bring him back to life.
Music of the Soul

And so in my seeking, in finding my guide, I did find Allah—not the full taste, but one big enough to fan the flame of my inherent but dormant yearning. It was enough to inflame my passion for the real tasting, enough to eventually let parts of me die so that I could be brought back, to live in greater accord with the way I was created to live. I have discovered a passion for Allah since knowing Sidi, and it has been nurtured and kept alive. Parts of me have died, but Sidi has shown me a new life.

Imagine a world in which all of the things you know suddenly disappear. There are no longer any landmarks for you to recognize as you go from one place to another. Maybe there are not even roads or cars, or any modern conveniences such as telephones or toilets. All our familiar ways of communicating are gone. This is kind of how it feels when you want to recreate a new life and have things that you've never had. We all have the power to create from what has not existed before, from the formless divine matter. You can purchase land and build a new house, or you can tear down a house and rebuild a new one, just as I eventually learned from Sidi how to let go of my old life and allow Allah to guide me to a new creation. It all begins with the desire for change.

God's love and caring call to all of us. It is not His fault, but ours, that we don't always awaken to the sound of this calling. But if you weren't hearing this calling, you would not be reading this now. Without some sense of this calling, I would not have made it to Sidi. I wouldn't be writing this now. I would likely still be pursuing material dreams, still waiting to surrender to this calling.

> And he whom I have killed, I owe him a debt;
> And to the one that is owed, I become that which is owed.
> There is no difference between Me and him
> Because I am he and he is I.

Music of the Soul

When we lie down and surrender to God, when we prostrate with all our being, when we allow our arrogance to turn into humility, when we let go of pride and accept our ignorance, when our material essence dies and we trust in our love— then we experience the grace written about here.

> *True prostration is complete surrender. Come in submission to Allah. Prostrate in the way of the angels. Prostrate with all your heart, because this is where Allah sits. This is the house of your Lord. Prayer must have prostration in the heart, total submission. See everyone as a manifestation of Allah and annihilate into the qualities of Allah. This is the real pardon of our sins: to know that, when we die and our sins are forgiven, we are reunited with the source of our being, and a truer, more real unity is experienced. We see with a different eye, hear with a different ear, feel with a different heart.*

As Sidi writes in *Music of the Soul:*

*This is the first part of the love in which Allah breathes all
the creation into existence, and the second part of the love is
the return in which the creature breathes his existence back
into his Lord.*

**Now we are ready to start the real walking, in the right
direction—protected and led by the guide, who has had the
true taste, who lives the real life, and who invites us to
share of his heart and his knowing. He is the bridge. He
lays himself at our feet so that we may see in his surrender
what is needed of us to cross.** For those of you who know
Sidi: Have you ever thought about why he always sits and
sleeps on the floor? It is not just to model the way of the
prophet, may peace and blessings be upon him, but to be an
example of the humility of a true prostration. Not only do we
sit at his feet when he teaches, he is sitting at ours.

Sidi has told us many times of when he was with his guide.
Having displayed some arrogance, he was asked to care for
the shoes of all the other beloveds, which he did for a long
time. Sidi cooks and serves his beloveds, and lives to help
them in their walking. If the guide is willing to do these
things, should it not be an example for us all? Here, in Sidi's
own words, is a teaching about humility, from a talk given to
beloveds:

*Once my shaykh said to me, "Your job is to look after the
shoes of your brothers." So my job for a year and a half was
to take care of the shoes, to cook and serve the food, to clean
the zawiyah, and to take care of the brothers. I listened with*

my ears and my heart to all instructions. After two years he told me to sit by his side, staying in the adab with my brothers, so there should be no difference between me and my brothers in the zawiyah. What is the reason for serving them by caring for their shoes? Because I was a young man, a strong man, a tough kid. So the shaykh said these nafs needed to be taken care of. So this was my first teaching, the first teaching for my nafs, so that I would learn honesty and more to care for others. This is what filled me with mercy and fear and love for all people without distinction. So this is the first step of walking from this world to another.

You have seven heavens and seven earths. You need to carry the love, and carry the goodness to every one who wrongs you. Be sincere and be truthful and you will find happiness. Clean your heart so it contains mercy, love and compassion. Clean your heart by believing and following every order that God sent through his prophets. Do not make any differences between any of them or any of the holy books because every word has a very deep meaning. It is just that many people do not understand. The Bible has been edited, changed and translated so many different ways that some of the things that were said are not exactly as they were stated. But people don't need a set of rules from outside but a true inner guidance system, based on the truths from the prophets. Look inward and find the holy essence of your heart and the truth it contains. To clean your heart you must remember the name at all times. Allah has greater knowledge of ourselves than we have. Migrate to a more subtle humanity because your vision is not complete if you stop with your body.

During the summer of 2003, Noorudeen Durkee, the first
westerner to have prolonged contact with Sidi, visited with
him quite a lot and helped teach the beloveds about the path.
Later, in a conversation I had with him, he explained one of
the things that showed him who Sidi was. He happened to
see Sidi open his suitcase to get some papers, and had a
chance to look inside. He saw that Sidi had absolutely
nothing but the papers, so there was, in essence, no baggage
at all. I am deeply blessed to have traveled with Sidi for
years, and I always carry a lot of "stuff" in my case. It is
interesting that, most of the time, I don't use my "stuff." Yet I
continue to carry it. I am always in a station of fear that Sidi
will ask for something to be done, and I will need certain
tools to do it, so I want to be prepared. I would probably do
better to trust that I don't need those things, that I carry
within me all that is needed to accomplish any task he might
ask of me. So when Noorudeen saw there was nothing in the
case, it was a telling example in many ways.

I am still weighed down by more stuff than I need, and have
not gotten to the point where I've let it all go. I do feel that
I'm not nearly as attached to things as I once was, though I
have a thousand pretty good excuses for why certain things
are still in my life—but in my heart I know they will not
bring me deeper into my essence or closer to knowing Allah.

I spent the better part of that first full day in Jerusalem
fluctuating between the inspired state I reached through
reading and writing the teachings, and concern about how I
would feel when I next saw Sidi. I remember now that, at one

point, I went out with Maryam to get a notebook to write the teachings in, and we went to the market for food. Maryam made simple meals, and I remember thinking how good it all tasted, even though I didn't have a big appetite. After a few short hours of being in Jerusalem, I was starting to appreciate simpler things.

The "difference between me and Him" was starting to lessen, after years of what appeared to be stagnation. Maybe things were moving more than I knew, even though I wasn't aware of it. Maybe I needed to get to the end of the road I was on before I could summon the strength to change direction. We can start to change things by first believing them to be different. When we change the way we look at things and react to them, then the things we are looking at change.

When we start to touch even the borders of the unity with Allah through conscious awareness, the comings and goings are dissolved into the experience of leaving what we thought we loved, only to discover there is another kind of love. It would be years before I had a strong enough sense of this love to let go of the other kind of love. But even though I didn't know it at the time, I was on my way.

When we learn to swim in the ocean of this love, to drink from it, it is intoxicating. This is the "wine" the Sufis refer to, for drinking alcohol is not permitted by the Koran. Yet no alcohol or drug in the world compares to this intoxication. **Just as no material food can satisfy the inner hunger, no amount of drugs or alcohol can replace the divine nectar.**

We learn in *The Secret of the Love of God* that "the basis of love is knowledge, and the basis of knowledge is existence." As we start to know the true essence of another, we start to realize our own true self, and this is the real knowledge. It is through loving that our knowing comes about, and it is from this love and the knowing of this love that existence springs into being.

In *Music of the Soul,* we learn that we are one with Allah. Thus, we are existence, and there is nothing contained in existence except Allah: **"The human being in its dense form is distinguishable from God, but the image of the human being eventually disappears as we are extinguished in the fire of the passion of our himma. We return to our initial reality, before we were born; and we are without form, or color, without any dimension, without any sex, male or female. We dissolve all the outside forms as we are dissolved in the unity of the one true God."**

When we are blessed to know this kind of love—through tasting with another beloved, through loving a child (or even an animal), or through surrender to the guide, and the profound and unconditional love one can feel for him—it makes the possibility of unity more easy to imagine. **I think this teaching says that we are reaching out to love ourselves when we seek to love another. We want to once again feel the peace of unconditional love, which is how God loves us all. And when we love ourselves, it is God loving Himself—so His purpose in creating mankind, to know the deep and secret essence of Himself, is realized.**

Repentance

The next teaching that caught my attention was *The Stations of the Way*. The first message that came through to me strongly was that there is no way to walk through these stations without Allah's grace and the help of the guide. This made complete sense to me and, as the years have gone by, I have come to know that it is true for me. There were moments when, in my arrogance, I thought I didn't need anyone to show me how to live or how to go to God. Many seekers before me had found God, or at least claimed to, and said they had done it on their own. And if they could do it, I could do it. Sidi teaches that we must walk through all the stations, and that he sends his heart and spirit to help us with this walking.

I felt that, when Sidi says he gives us his heart to travel through the stations, he is totally truthful. I could feel the immense, limitless generosity of his love through his writings. I could feel him within my heart as I started to read the stations.

I was aware of the stations because I had read other Sufi texts, but I had never paid such close attention. Sidi clearly said that, if you can open your heart completely, you can walk, or move, through the stations quickly. If you give everything in one day, Allah will give you everything in one day; if you give everything in one hour, Allah will give you everything in one hour. The first time I read this statement, I hoped to move from the place where I was stuck, into one of less pain, pretty quickly. I failed to take proper notice of the part where he said, "This is very difficult." I registered the second part of the phrase, "…but at the same time very easy." I look at that now and wonder, *Easy for whom?*

I had another illusion: that once you walk through a particular station you are done with it. This came back to humble me many times. First, I had no idea of how much it took to give everything to Allah for even one moment, much less sustain it for one hour, or one day. It would take some time before it hit me—hard—that opening my heart to that extent would take serious work, and a depth of surrender that I felt far from.

In *The Stations of the Way,* Sidi refers to 28 stations. There are seven stations of the self (an-nafs), seven stations of the heart, seven stations of the soul, and seven stations of the secret. As I read through the stations my nafs was strong: I wanted to rush to the end of the teaching, to reach the understanding of the secret he was referring to. I decided to speed-read through the writings, get the general gist, and then go back and write them. I honestly was arrogant enough to think that, if I read everything, I would reach a state of enlightenment about the stations even before Sidi came back later in the day. My self (my nafs) was telling me that this would impress him concerning the sincerity of my seeking. I didn't know at that time how transparent I was to him, but I can assure you I know it now.

I thought that, because I understood the principles behind what he was sharing, I had reached that particular station. So if I felt I had reached a certain station in the seven stations of the secret, this also meant I had traversed the other stations up to that point, and was done with them. True to the writing, I felt I was traveling through everything in an instant—but nothing could have been further from the truth.

Sidi quotes the Koran in *The Path to Allah Most High*: "The higher levels of the stations are more perfect expressions of the infinite and divine love. Each level is more refined and more expansive. And those that arrive see no imperfections. The highest truth is that I alone am." (20:9-39)

For years afterward, I was caught in some kind of game, always asking Sidi what station I was in. I realize now that, by asking, I placed myself clearly in the first two stations of the nafs: that of listening to the orders from the darkness, and that of still questioning. I am humbled by his patience, by the gentle way he held these questions and basically fed these states of my nafs. He did not admonish me, but gave me lots of rope to hang myself with, so to speak. There were many times he gave me clues to what I was doing, but I was adept at filtering out any information that diminished how holy I thought myself to be. **Even the prophets have had the shaitan whisper in their ears, so it is kind of ludicrous that I thought I was above this. I think the more Allah calls to you, the more of the whispers you will become aware of. But with Allah and the guide, you have inside you what is necessary to develop resistance to this whispering.**

Even in the beginning of the first station, we are taught to remember the name of Allah, to pray and continue to study the teachings so that we may move forward. These practices are necessary and recommended, no matter where you think you are in your walking.

Maryam came back into my room, and told me it was time to pray. She asked if I would like to pray with her. She said that if I hadn't made wudu (ablution), I should do it. I was too proud and embarrassed to tell her I didn't know how to make a proper wudu, so I went into the bathroom, splashed water all over myself, and came back out for prayer. I watched as she made her salat, but this time she was silent, so all I could do was follow her movements. I remember being impatient to get back to the teachings, and feeling like I was wasting time. I have often asked for Allah's forgiveness around this aspect of my character.

It is not particularly pleasant for me to reveal these parts of myself, but I want you to know who I was and where I was in my walking. I hope that, in a way, you will realize how helpless and foolish I was, and that my experience will serve as an example of the mercy and compassion of the guide and Allah.

As my mind wandered while my body followed Maryam's movements, I experienced my own emptiness. I was ashamed that I wasn't moved by the prayer, and that I was too embarrassed to ask her to teach me the wudu. I realize now that all I did was put myself in a corner of my own making.

These imperfections created a lot of veils that kept me from understanding and seeing clearly the meaning of Sidi's teachings—so I prevented myself from being able to move forward in a more honest way. I was lying to others who wanted to help me by withholding some of what I thought, and I was the one who lost the most because of this.

Even today, this part of my personality is apparent to me. When someone asks if I know something, my tendency is to say yes, even if I don't. But I am learning to catch myself, and am at least able to ask someone something without feeling shame. I might feel embarrassed, but that I can deal with and accept. I don't like hiding behind shame.

Now, years after having started my walk with Sidi, I still find parts of myself in the first two stations (listening to the orders from the darkness, and questioning). I have learned that, if one part of you goes through a station, it doesn't mean you don't ever come back to it. There are stations within stations. Maybe not all aspects of your being have gone through a station, or through all parts of it. After the nafs of the material self are looked at, we get to look at the nafs of our spiritual being. How often in my life have I felt that I am better than someone else because I do certain spiritual practices? How often has a part of me looked at someone else with judgment about how they live their life? How often have I felt superior because I knew something someone else didn't? I still ask forgiveness from Allah for these thoughts; I still ask Sidi to guide me so that my nafs disappear from my life; I still try to avoid going to these places.

This is one of the tremendous benefits of the teachings around the stations. Once we have walked in awareness, consciously in a station, it becomes easier to recognize it when we fall back into it. Sometimes we can think we are in one station, unaware of the fact that we are predominantly stuck in a different one. I think we are never in just one station. As there are many different parts of our being, we touch many stations simultaneously. So while I might recognize that I am having an experience similar to one described in the stations of the secret, I may also have unresolved issues from a station in the nafs.

I now remember going out with Maryam to get the notebook. We walked awhile, and then took a bus to the old city, where we walked through the souks (markets) to get our supplies. I had lived for around 25 years in France, and had been many times to Morocco and other countries; I had always loved the atmosphere of the souks. I saw so many amazing faces as I walked with Maryam; I thought about not having my camera with me, and all the portraits I was missing. But I took the photos in my mind's eye, and they are still with me now. As I run through the images in my imagination, the sounds and smells come back as well, and it feels as if I am again walking through the markets, following Maryam, who is just a few steps ahead of me. I am amazed at the dexterity she shows as she bustles through the crowded alleys, how much strength she has in her tiny frame, and how resourceful she is. When going out she always wore the hijab, the headdress worn by Muslim women. She had such an elegance about her, and blended right in with all the other women on the street.

Looking at the happy and smiling faces of the people there, I realized how poor I was. Here were a people at war, living in a terrible economy, earning barely enough to survive (if they were lucky), and they still could smile. I was actually jealous. I had a lot of questions. *Why is all this pain in my heart? What did I do wrong? How am I going to move on from this terrible mess I am in?*

And I realize now that this was the perfect example of the first two stations of the nafs. I wanted to get back to the zawiyah and copy more of the teachings. I wanted to start filling the notebook I had bought. I wondered if I should recopy what I put on paper in the morning, so that everything would be organized nicely in the notebook...I had other rather frivolous and unnecessary thoughts. I did not realize there were lessons in the souk for me, just as important as those in the zawiyah. I grew impatient to get back, and I felt fatigued from lack of sleep.

It says in the holy Koran: "For God guides to His light the one who wills to be guided." (Surah an Nur 24:35) I wanted to be guided. All the cells of my being seemed to be crying for help, for some kind of answer to alleviate the pressure of my depression.

When Maryam and I returned to the zawiyah, I continued to write the stations, finishing the seven stations of the nafs and moving into the stations of the heart. I understood the last five stations of the nafs, but did not feel I had any of the quiet or the peace that is mentioned in these teachings. I could still hear the incessant voice of the shaitan, and could feel the pull of the material world. I felt far from having been purified.

But when I started writing the first station of the heart—*At-Tawba*, or *The Return to God*—I could feel something start to move inside me. I think, by Allah's grace, I have always been able to feel deeply in my heart and have been a sensitive person. And I have almost always trusted the intuition and instincts I have experienced through my feelings. One of the reasons I took good pictures was that I followed my feelings. So a lot of the awareness I had came through what I felt in my heart.

I remembered seeing another teaching about at-tawba, so I looked through the papers for it. I didn't start to write this one because I wanted to keep all the stations in order. (I guess that was the part of me that likes certain things to be organized, and was still caught up in appearances.) But I immediately and instinctively knew that the words I was reading provided one of the answers I was looking for. **First, it said, you have to feel grieved and sorry for what you have done before. You have to find and surrender to the guide, to the heir of the Muhammadan presence, and to follow everything he tells you. I absolutely knew by now that I had found the person who was the guide.** I had been educated in what were supposed to be the best schools in the country, had even been to Yale for a while, but I could not begin to express the knowledge revealed in these teachings. I learned that tawba (repentance) is the first stage for admission and for making peace with God. From wherever Sidi sourced his information, I knew it was what I needed, and this teaching confirmed everything with an exclamation mark.

The teaching explained what had happened the night before, when I had put my hand in Sidi's, promising to accept him as my spiritual father and follow the Shaddhuli way—the way of the love, the peace, the mercy and the justice. I promised to follow the way of the prophets, of Abraham and Moses and Jesus. (Sidi teaches that the light of Allah was so strong that only the prophets contained this light.) Then when I had proclaimed the shahadah and become a Muslim by saying, *Ash-hadu ana la ilaha illa'llah, wa ash-hadu anna Muhammadan rasul Allah*—there is no God but God and Muhammad is the prophet of God—I started a whole new phase of my life. I now spend my life praying that I can say this cleanly and purely, and entirely from my heart. Sidi says the shahada is a way to bring all your limbs to conform to Allah. First, you realize in your heart what you are expressing; then the limbs start to conform to that understanding.

Sidi has said that *la ilaha illa'llah* contains every secret and everything that is known; it is the highest form of remembrance, revealed or unrevealed. The prophet, may peace and blessings be upon him, said in a hadith, "I have brought nothing more important than the shahadah." When the shahadah is accepted sincerely, the result is the surrender (islam) to God and becoming Muslim.

I needed to clean my heart of the rust around it, if I wanted to have a clear reflection of Allah. The rust that covered my heart was the feelings of anger, hatred and jealousy I was experiencing. I resented the men my wife was seeing; I resented my wife for seeing them; I was possessive and selfish in wanting her for myself. None of these feelings did anything good for me, but they added a lot of dirt to the mirror of my heart. An appetite for the things of the material world will create rust, as will wanting anything other than Allah. **Just as a mirror will not reflect a clear image if it is rusty or covered with dust, the heart cannot reflect the clear light of revelation if it is covered with desire for things of the world.**

I was to learn that anger, resentment, jealousy, hatred and other similar emotions were really low energies that weakened you in the long run. Love, gratitude, acceptance, forgiveness and similar emotions are positive energies that reflect more connection with divine love. There is an endless supply of all qualities from the source of creation, and it is up to us which ones we want to use.

In reality, when my hand was in Sidi's hand, I was following the order of Allah, who said, "Those who give you the promise are actually giving the promise to Me. When you put your hand with his hand, it is My hand." The hand of God is over the hand of Sidi, and *Music of the Soul* explained that if ever I broke the covenant I had made with him, I would break my promise with Allah. I felt something open in my heart at that moment—only for an instant, but it felt so special. When you touch the hand of a beloved, you both touch eternity.

The teaching went on to say that, after taking this promise, I would stand at the gate; to enter, I must be repentant. This is one of the meanings of tawba: It refers to a return to something…the leaving of certain things and acceptance of others. By repenting, I could clean myself of past sins. For many years I had heard the message of being damned and going to hell because of my sins. So this was a clear, heartwarming message that gave me hope—which was one thing I desperately needed.

Here was what I had been thinking about all day: *What could I do now to help alleviate the pain in my heart?* Sidi explained that there are three stages of repentance. **The first is to be ready and willing to leave the past behind, and to feel grieved by what you have done before.** If I stayed focused on the past, I could not be "the son of my moment." I had to ask God's forgiveness for my sins, intentional and unintentional. I had to say I was sorry for everyone I had hurt, even for the pain I had caused without knowing it. If I stayed focused on the past, I would put up a wall between who I was and who I wanted to become. I was to surrender everything to Allah, and ask for His mercy and forgiveness. My understanding was that, if my asking was authentic and my repentance was heartfelt and honest, I would be forgiven. I did feel bad about my past; I did feel sorry for many of the things I had done. In fact, I felt ashamed.

Suddenly, I got a glimpse of a new life. I didn't see myself going to hell at death; I felt I could wipe the slate clean and start a new life. I couldn't sustain that feeling—but I recognized the promise I had started to feel, in having found Sidi, for the blessing it was.

A hadith says, "In the body there is a piece of meat; if this is right, the whole body will be right; and if this is bad, the whole body will be bad; and this piece of meat is the heart." The heart is the house of Allah. But it can also be the house of the devil, so it is necessary to clean the heart of things like jealousy and hatred, which were taking a big place in mine. Sidi has spoken to beloveds:

> *Allah makes revelations in the heart of His creation. When a beloved cleans himself completely, this is the manifestation of the revelation. That revelation in its deepest sense is the one apparent characteristic that Allah gives us. If you follow, then your senses, your consciousness and your heart will rest from anxiety and fatigue. What will remain is the best of manners. Sit on the rug of happiness. First the tongue, heart and organ manifest every action. Faith circulates from the heart to every cell. What is alive in one's heart, one's mind cannot articulate or define. You have to eat the fruit to taste it.*

> *The sickness of the body can be helped and healed by medicine, but the heart needs to be healed through loving and surrendering to Allah.*

It is not our wealth that will bring us into the presence of Allah, but our actions and intentions, and the purity of our hearts. My previous focus on creating security and impressing others through my material possessions was, in fact, adding a lot of rust to my heart. I needed a radical shift of intention if I was to find my way along this path. I could feel I was ready to surrender many things, as holding on to them had only gotten me to where I was. In a way, I felt lucky that something worse hadn't happened. I have read in the Koran that, if you cannot be grateful for what you have—which I was not in a state of acceptance to do—then at least be thankful for what you have escaped. I don't know how aware I was of it at that time, but I do know I felt not only ready, but ripe, for these teachings.

The second condition of repentance is that you must stop doing bad things immediately. You must be ready to turn to the guide and to Allah, and make the intention to lead a cleaner life. I know there have been more than a few times, such as the experience in Paris, when I've promised God anything if He would only get me through a certain situation. I remember a long time ago, when a young girl told me she might be pregnant, I pleaded with God: If only she weren't pregnant, I would never sleep with another girl again. I did not keep this intent, but I could see that in moments of truth I had been willing.

Now I would have to keep such promises intact and, as I had tasted the willingness pretty strongly before, I figured all I had to do now was keep my promises. **The prophet, peace and blessings be upon him, said in a hadith: "Whoever wants Allah to answer his call in hard times, let him plead to Allah in easy times."** I didn't want to repent from fear of what would happen if I didn't, or because of some reward I might get if I did. I wanted to come to repentance through a real and genuine desire to know God, which the teaching clearly shared was the best way.

To genuinely ask for forgiveness, we should do so with our whole heart, body, mind and soul. Each one of our senses should be surrendered to Allah. Thus it becomes a lot more than uttering a few words with our tongue. As we grow in awareness, we are held more and more responsible for our promises and commitments.

In Sidi's words, here is what I mentioned before: "God has said, 'My slaves, if you didn't sin, I would have created others who sin, so that when they sin, they will ask forgiveness. And I will give them forgiveness because I am the forgiver and the merciful.'" I admit to being uncomfortable the first few times I saw the word slave. I had always thought of slavery as what we were exposed to in this country when white people "owned" black slaves, and I was never comfortable with the idea. But the slave Sidi teaches about is different. The word "slavehood" ('ubudiyya) is derived from the verb "to worship" ('abada), and this is the pure and essential quality of the slave. **Sidi constantly tells us, "I am a poor slave for Allah." So when we surrender to the guide, we surrender to Allah because, when the guide is the perfect slave, there is nothing inside him except Allah.**

Being a slave for Allah means that one carries the qualities of Allah and does not move without His order. There is no separation between any of Allah's creations, so the slave is there to serve everyone, without distinction. The station of slave is a high one, because the true slave is living always in the station of the unity.

Sidi always encourages us to keep company with the lovers of Allah, and to draw on the inspiration of those who are committed to the walking. When you keep company with the true lovers of Allah, you are, because of their slavehood, keeping company with Allah.

"Oh our Lord, forgive us and we know our end is unto you." Sidi says,

> This creed is the creed of all the messengers and there is no differentiation between any of the noble messengers. This is the message of the true Islam, not the Islam that is understood by some people. The true Islam is the message of love, peace, mercy, justice and freedom. Neither Islam nor Allah teach killing. The real Islam prohibits that which is bad. The sacred laws protect the heart of Islam, just as the bark protects a tree. Islam teaches that all people are brothers and sisters, giving the love to each other, not killing or destroying or stealing from each other, or exploiting others, or having enmity or envy. They live in the love, in cooperation with each other. As for those who go outside the order of Allah, regardless of whether they are Christians or Jews or claiming to be Muslims, if they commit acts of violence and kill or steal or exploit, these are not believers and are only rebellious shaytans (devils). The real Islam, as we

know, is the Islam of Abraham and the Islam of Moses and the Islam of Jesus. Is Jesus not the Messenger of peace? Is he not the Messenger of the mercy? Is he not the Messenger of justice? Did Moses not receive the Torah with the 10 commandments? Do not steal. Do not kill. These are to be found in the Bible and the Quran. Why? Because they are one message. The people who make separation between the Messengers are not the people of Allah. Those who attack others are not from the family of Allah.

There is no separation between black and white, male and female. All of you are brothers and sisters. All of you are from the earth. Your father is Adam and your mother is Eve. No human is better than another or should regard himself as better. The only difference [between people] is in what works are offered by each for the welfare of humanity. What goodness, love, security, mercy, justice, freedom, and help is given. Those who help the poor, oppressed and sick are engaging in right action. Allah wants us to show compassion towards those who suffer. It is our duty. When you lead a life in which you share love and happiness with people, you will be surprised at how happy you will be. Do not take over the wealth of others. Do not kill others.

How many hearts have you seen that are broken? Why? Because people are not walking within the orders of Allah. They go with their passion and they lose themselves, because they have broken the love. Love is the basis for everything. The prophet, may the peace and blessings of Allah be upon him, says to us, "Follow me and Allah will

love you." If you follow the divine orders you become
worthy of receiving love; then you are able to give love in
the right way. Do not give love in the wrong way. It is not
permissible. It is important to obey every order. You need to
place everything in the way Allah wants it—not in the way
that your nafs may want it or how the shaytan wants it.
Obedience to your nafs is disobedience to Allah and
obedience to the shaytan.

There is a hadith that says we can experience happiness simply by gazing upon the true slave of Allah. When I spend months traveling with Sidi to different places, I feel this sense of happiness and inspiration. As the years go on, I can summon those feelings without his physical presence. How many days have I sat by his side, and been amazed at the profound connection and deep awareness that is present at all times in him? And I feel how all the beloveds are renewed in their commitment when he is around.

The third condition of repentance is that you must be ready to completely abandon doing bad things any more. The way to move beyond intent is to surrender to the guide and deepen one's commitment to the practices: doing the five daily prayers, practicing remembrance, developing asceticism (withdrawing the senses, and not surrendering to material desires), following the shari'a (the laws of Islam), and giving zakat (tithing and caring for the poor). There are many other ways. We also are taught the meaning of the sacrifice asked of and made by Abraham, which is a deep ritual, through which we can approach a true atonement.

The seven nafs of each station are one, but they are named differently so we can more understand their attributes. We are asked to be more aware of ourselves now: to pay closer attention to the things within us that create challenges, and that draw us away from the cleansing of the heart and the outpouring of the love. We are prisoners of our nafs in these stations, because it can control us and lead us astray. During those days in Jerusalem, I was in a prison of my own making, dominated by fear and controlled by my emotions. It would be a long time before I would find solace and peace by repeating the name. When I think about how much more quickly I could have walked the path, by simply letting go rather than trying to control everything, by starting and learning the practices, I am in a bit of wonderment at my own stupidity.

Today, we are blessed because there are many beloveds walking the path who can help the student move faster; so many who have gone much faster than I did, who can understand and teach the practices, and who have truly given of themselves to share this path with others. I imagine that, at one time or another, many of them went through an extremely painful, deeply personal battle, and that they wrestled with their own demons. **But as you move deeper, through these early stations, the fear is released. The constrictions will turn into expansion; the anger, resentment and other lesser emotions, and our animal tendencies, will turn into loving and nurturing expressions of life. You will start to experience a freedom that is a celebration of life.** In these stations you can use fear positively; it is not always negative.

Fear that we are ruining our environment has pushed many people to a point of awareness that can help correct this situation. So a fear that you are hopeless without the guide and Allah can be used to turn your life around.

During the prayer we prostrate ourselves numerous times. One thing this prostration does for me is remind me many times each day of the beauty of feeling and being humble. I was humbled by the time I got to Sidi. I felt poor and diminished, in relation to all the knowing he communicated in his teachings. I know now that I could not lift a pinky finger if Allah did not allow it. The human being is nothing without Allah, for we cannot make an ant or the petal of a flower or a dewdrop, or anything of this world, without His aid.

A funny story that someone sent me over the Internet illustrates this:

There were three scientists who learned how to clone human beings, so they decided they didn't need God anymore. They elected one of the three to go see God, and give Him the news.

So one of the scientists went to God and said, "We want to thank you for helping us get this far, but we want to make a go of it on our own now. So I just wanted to come and thank you on behalf of the three of us before we said goodbye."

"No problem," said God. "But before you go, let's have a little man-making contest."

"I would like that," responded the scientist.

And God replied, "Let's make him from before the time Adam existed."

This prevented the scientist from using anything from a human body.

"No problem," said the scientist, and he knelt down and scooped up a handful of dirt.

"Oh no," said God. "You have to use your own dirt."

Without God we are nothing, and nothing can be done without Him. We are helpless and hopeless, as far as I am concerned. We are creations of God, with an inherent potential for divinity, and full of unlimited possibilities.

I would have to give up my old, limited self, surrender what I thought was control of my life, and trust the heart of the guide. I had no idea of the territory I was entering, or the degree of desperation I would still feel. I was a long way from sustaining any of the rays of hope I was experiencing. I hadn't even seen Sidi the second time, and I was still wondering if I would recognize him when I did.

Who is the Guide?

I was starting to feel impatient to see Sidi again. Many questions and thoughts had popped into my mind, and I wanted to know the answers now, not tomorrow. I couldn't even remember the name he had given me; without Maryam there to remind me, I would have fit "to a t" the picture of *he is so lost he doesn't even know his own name.* Here I was, the father of four kids, a successful photographer, a man of the world—and I was as helpless as a newborn baby.

In a talk to beloveds, Sidi has said that the messenger of Allah said: "Leave the dunya to its people. If anyone takes from the dunya any more than he needs, he is hurting himself without realizing it."

I had taken more than my share, but I was rapidly growing aware of how I had hurt myself. During this time, I was a slave to my possessions, rather than a slave for Allah. **"Do not be a slave to the material world," Sidi says. "Let the material world be your slave."** Just meeting the expenses of my lifestyle would take every drop of my energy, and use valuable time I could have spent developing the practices. At that time, in that moment, I would have given just about everything I had in the material world to ease the pain. I didn't know the real problem: that I wasn't ready to give up everything. Too much of me still thought comfort and protection would come from outside of me, rather than from developing more inner strength. Oh, a part of me thought I could give it all up—but my nafs (my self) was not going to surrender that easily.

While a part of my world had shrunken to the small room in which I sat and wrote the teachings, my universe was opening and expanding to show me things I had dreamed of, but never experienced. I didn't understand what had happened the night before. I didn't consciously understand what I had done in taking Sidi's hand, but it felt right. Though I was not familiar with many things about Islam, I had been attracted to the Arab culture for decades. My house was filled with rugs, chairs, fabrics, paintings, shelves, wooden plaques with writings from the Koran—all from the Arab countries I had visited. I also had a huge library of books by many different Sufis, including volumes of the teachings of Hazrat Inayat Khan, which I had read and reread. So I knew what it was about in my *heart*, more than I could explain with my mind.

I don't remember if I had been writing for minutes or hours when Sidi appeared to say hello. He was returning from his day of work at the mosque and, fortunately, I knew right away that it was him. I think it was his spirit that I recognized, and the power that poured from him. It was not yet dark when he joined us; he went to sit on the mattress, on the floor in the room next to where I had been sleeping and writing the teachings. Maryam went to make tea, and we were left alone.

How are you, Salih?

I wondered if he was using the new name to talk to a new part of me.

"I've been busy, Sidi, writing the teachings."

Which ones did you write?

My mind was in such a confused state, I couldn't even remember the names of the teachings I had written—so I told him I was now writing the stations, and that it was bringing up many things for me. (Many times I have sat before Sidi, and gotten completely tongue-tied. Even today, if he wants, he can make my mind go blank, and I will forget everything I meant to ask him. I have realized that questions are by invitation only.)

"What am I going to do, Sidi? I feel like I'm dying."

Trust Allah. He loves you more than you love yourself.

I sat in the silence, looking for words to share my heart with him. In the next few days, I would spend more time in my dark mind—formulating questions instead of listening to what he was telling me and taking the answers into my heart. I stared into his eyes, and he looked into my soul. I didn't need to say a word. He knew me better than I knew myself; he knew everything I was going through.

Maryam brought the tea, and sat with us in the silence. I remembered the night before, when Sidi had called the angels. After he had written the Koranic phrases on her hand, she went into a kind of trance; as an angel spoke through her, she wrote on paper the answers to many questions I had asked. I had read them many times. Every word rang true. My questioning mind wondered how these answers could be on those papers; neither of them knew me at all. There were so many things that transcended my understanding. Nathalie was not there in the flesh, but her spirit must have been visible, because the papers correctly described everything about her in detail.

I asked Sidi the meaning of my name, and the meaning of what had happened the night before. I asked him what I had done wrong and why Nathalie had run away. He gave me answers I could contain.

This is not from your hand. You must be patient and trust Allah. You must be the earth for your holy children.

The tea burned my tongue and the pain burned my heart.

You will have to be patient, my love. Everything will come in Allah's time.

"But what can I do now Sidi? I feel so lost. I can't sleep; I can't eat; sometimes I can't even breathe."

Read and write the teachings, my son. Learn to repeat the name. All the answers are with Allah and from Allah. You must cross and learn to trust.

"What do you mean by cross?" I asked.

Leave the old and come to the new. Your old ways won't work anymore. You must let all the old thoughts go and trust that this holy way is the real food that you have been looking for.

Trust, trust, trust…Trust was the litany. I was thinking: *If I can't trust myself, how can I trust anything else?* I had no idea about anything, especially any kind of solution. I looked at Sidi and wondered if I was grasping at straws. Yet this was just the dark mind; most of me recognized this was the real thing and that, even though I didn't fully know it, I was finally on a safe shore.

I decided that, the next time I had a chance, I would look more closely at the teachings about the guide, so I would be better prepared the next time I sat with him. I felt insecure in not knowing him, while I could tell he knew me. I knew what I wanted from him: I wanted him to give me comfort, and all the knowledge and tools I would need to combat my nafs, as well as the depression that focusing on my self had led to. **But I have learned that, though Sidi doesn't always give you what you think you want, he does give you what you can carry at the time.**

At that time, though I didn't know it, I wasn't ready to carry much. I couldn't carry the whole truth of my responsibility for what had happened; I couldn't carry the whole truth of the outcome; I couldn't carry the whole truth of my own attachments. So from his mercy and compassion, Sidi contained me and held me in his heart. He gave me love and understanding and guidance that were beyond my ability to understand at that time.

Sidi spoke to me gently, caressing my heart with his love. He said that I had now come to drink from the real ocean, the ocean that held the water of the real medicine. He said he lived for those who sought this water, who wanted to know and wanted to walk for their beloved God in this world. Thus, he was ready to open the door for everyone who is thirsty to walk in this way, because there is no life for anyone without the love of Allah.

> *I tell you now that you must always be with your beloved God and to trust him and to not stop with any pictures. Be strong, Salih, and trust Allah. Know how to use everything He gives you in the right way, and be wise, before everything and after everything.*

He also told me I should be grateful because Allah had given me a pure heart, and had opened the door for me and accepted me as one of His children. He quoted the Hadith Qudsi: "In the body there is a heart; in the heart there is what is hidden, and in what is hidden there is what is more hidden, and in the more hidden there is a secret, and in the secret I am. Know that there is no God except me, so worship me and establish the prayer in my remembrance." Sidi went on:

> *Do not think that you are a small star. The larger universe is enveloped within you. You carry the whole universe.*

When you carry the message you carry the responsibility,
so carry what you promise to carry with your promise, and
protect the hearts of your children that are placed in your
care.

This is all I can remember from that conversation, which was
not that long. He got up to leave and said he would return
later. He told me to continue writing the stations and to not
worry. Worry is forged in idle moments, so if I could keep
remembering the name, I would worry less. Activity is the
enemy of thought.

He was to repeat many times the words he spoke to me that
afternoon—until I was finally able to open my heart, and
accept them with an understanding that would change my
life forever. I am still astounded by the immense patience he
showed me over the years, never seeming to get angry or
frustrated when I would call him again and again with the
same message.

So I went back to my room and started looking for the papers
that taught more about who he was. I found the Silsila, an
account of the line of people from whom he came, which
went right back to the holy prophet Muhammad, peace and
blessings be upon him. I found information about who the
guide was, and about the Shaddhuli tariqa, the Sufi order he
not only belonged to, but was the head of. I learned the
Shaykh was the Guide of this Sufi path, founded by Shaykh
Ali Abu-l-Hasan as-Shaddhuli in thirteenth-century Egypt.
And in his spirit he is the inheritor, from his guide and

master, Shaykh Abdu-r-Rahman Abu-r-Risah of Halab in Syria, of the entire Shaddhuli tariqa.

His door is open to every seeker of the truth, and every person who seeks the healing he provides. He teaches that suffering is not of a material nature, but from a spiritual core; in order to heal our hearts of sickness, we must clean the rust, remove the veils, and reunite with our creator so that the love flows from us in the way that Allah loved His creation. In Sidi's words:

> *I am a very poor slave for Allah, and God, he gives me the permission to teach the people how to walk the way through the religion of unity, the religion of the prophet Muhammad, peace and blessings be upon him. This zawiyah is the zawiyah of the Shaddhuli Way. It is on the holy Mount of Olives. And I say to everyone, welcome. If he opens his heart, then I am ready to give him everything that he asks.*

> *If he wants to walk through the way to know Allah, to know how to be, and to clean his heart and carry the message of the peace and love and mercy and justice through the religion of the real Islam, then I am the slave for him. I teach him how to pray, and remember the name and how to make ablution.*

> *Be ready for everything that Allah wants from you to be. Open your heart completely and I will give you what you need, and what you can carry. First of all, write.*

*There is no separation between me and my beloved
students. I love them like I love myself, and they are the
children of God. He cares, and He asks me to care about
them. I am ready for everyone and I will give everything
that Allah He gives me for them.*

*Continue with the deep sincere and deep surrender and
trust, and I am sure God will give you everything you
need.*

Most of what I share with you now is the teachings that were
shown to me on that first trip, which had been collected from
the 1970s and are of a different flavor than those more
recently revealed. This is mostly due to the fact that Sidi had
many of these revelations written from dictations that he
made in English, rather than his native Arabic. Once Sidi
started teaching in Arabic, through interpreters, the lessons
became deeper and broader, as they flowed from his heart
and spirit toward the seeking beloveds.

In what I read that afternoon, I learned that it is important to
come to the guide with the proper politeness (adab), because
we are coming face to face with Allah, and the guide is the
one who carries this message. **Sidi is al-insan al-kamil, the
perfected one. This does not just mean he is perfect within
himself, but also that he can guide others to know perfection, because beloveds can use Sidi's presence as a mirror
that reflects their own potential back to them.** This awakens
a sleeping part within us and creates sparks, which he can
then fan into a fire that can clean our own hearts. We must

look deeply to see his qualities, and then be like him in these qualities.

The guide can help us when we meet the darkness of our nafs and our spirits are troubled. He understands every step we are taking and will take; he has been to the destination, and knows how to make a map to help us.

There are signs that will tell you if you have reached the guide. **His heart is the house of God, and he gives love to everyone. He works all the time, and he serves his beloveds with humility and devotion.** He does not waste time, and he gives everything he has to the poor. His own dunya life is irrelevant to him, and he lives to serve Allah and his beloveds. His time is Allah's time, and he uses it wisely. (His suitcase is empty.) People's skin color or culture is of no importance to him; all he sees is their hearts. His light shines upon everyone, and it is up to them to drink from his love, which is constant and never-ending.

He teaches everyone how to give by giving everything himself. There are layers upon layers behind every word he says, and the deep wisdom of Allah is behind every action. He can help us change our troublesome nafs into one having good qualities, and transform our anger and hate into love. I know he can do this because he helped me do it. **The Surah Muhammad in the holy Koran says: "And for those who respond to His guidance, He increases His guidance." I know that, as I responded to Sidi's guidance, he started to increase it, and I started to grow.** I started to see a deeper meaning behind everything he said, and that there was a lot more behind his actions than I initially thought.

The Shaddhuli tariqa is a path to Allah. During that first visit to Jerusalem, I asked Sidi to explain the difference between the religions, and his response was: "There is one religion, and it is surrender to God." Surah 3:15

Believe in your heart; assert the laws and principles of Islam from the depth of a living faith. Purify all your qualities; elevate them from the material, mundane world. Illuminate your way by the light of the prophet and guide. Increase your strength and your himma for your walking in order to realize proximity with Allah. Strengthen your relationship with Allah by making tawba. All this is a means to an end. The end is Allah.

*We must make tawba for claiming we have a self or existence, for the biggest sin is to think you have existence because you are making something of yourself besides Allah. Do not claim your attributes in the humanity. **An atom's worth of arrogance prohibits certain qualities. Beautify yourself with qualities beautiful to Allah.** Everything in heaven and earth begins with Allah. Can you stop sickness, death or create life? You have no claim of ownership. Let go of everything you claim to own and repent continuously.*

Know from where you were put in and taken out. Everyone, kings included, came through a channel (urinary tract), so

*why elevate yourself? We all come from the same water
(sperm), and who else can do this but Allah? Tawba gives
us hope. He created us to be free and to be in remembrance.
Why constrict yourself to your choices? Why are our eyes
in front of our head? (Don't turn right or left.)*

*Be always in prostration and in continual acts of worship.
The tawba is not from you, but Allah. The favor is from
Allah. Without Allah you have no tawba. Allah has chosen
the sincere ones to be His lovers. The nafs are our clothes of
grandeur. They come from earth and will return to earth. If
**He wanted a bad ending you would not have been
inspired to unity, so be inspired to unity and you will
see what you have never imagined from your heart.
There is no safety from Allah except to return to Him.***

*Allah is the just, the lover, the merciful, the compassionate.
He is the lover. He loves people. He ennobles people. We
need to surrender our affairs to Him. Islam is the total
surrender to Allah's orders. This is the real Islam, and it is
not the Islam where people kill people and destroy things.
When you live in the true Islam, you live in an ongoing
and everlasting garden in this world. It is for this that
Allah created the human being, not for suffering.*

*Allah wishes you to be happy. Submit to the guidelines,
hold the love always, follow the divine commandments,
practice sincerity and devotion when transacting with
others and trust Allah.*

I have seen many different spellings of *Shaddhuli,* such as Shadhiliyya and Shadhili. But though the letters might differ, the path is the same. We pray five times a day and we make dhikr (remembrance). You can read a more detailed description of Sufism, and of this path, in Sidi's books, which contain many of his teachings. My purpose here is not to paraphrase the teachings; it is to share with you how I have used some of them in my daily life, and how they can help you in your walking.

I feel it's necessary to follow the guide and to exercise trust, patience and faith in order to walk this path. There are many tests along the way; if you're looking for reasons to leave the path, they are easy to find. This is a straight path, but not always an easy one. **The teachings promise that, if you can surrender everything immediately (and I do mean everything), if you can feel total and full faith now, then you can enter the garden immediately. When we walk to Allah, He runs to us. When your faith is a true faith, then physical confirmation of the truth is not a necessity, for your mind does not question and your heart is open.**

As I read through all the explanations of the path and of the guide—through layer upon layer of congruent information—my belief in Sidi deepened. I was already starting to trust from a place deep in my heart. My mind was still playing games, questioning, struggling; but my heart, which Sidi had told me to trust, was opening more and more to him. **For God guides to His light the one who wills to be guided. (Surah an Nur 24:35)**

I wanted to be guided; of this I was sure. I not only wanted Sidi to take me to Allah, I *needed* him to take me there. I was at the end of the road I had been traveling. It took years to give up my old ways, and even though some tendencies probably still remain with me now, I do feel as if I have a new creation.

Even going back and reliving these moments is difficult, because I feel I am not being the son of my moment. It's also not a lot of fun to revisit all this dysfunction. But if it can help one person sustain their walking, I thank Allah—and I will continue, while holding this thought.

This story began during the most depressing and difficult time of my life. As it continues, I find myself arriving in the greatest garden I have ever known. **This is the garden Sidi says is the paradise of the presence of the unity of God.** I don't claim to be in the garden, but I feel myself arriving at a place where I can have the taste.

Sometimes, in order to love God, one has to give up what one loves most. We have to surrender some things we hold very dear. I had felt for years that I gave a lot to God. I thought about God a lot; I sought Him fairly consistently. Yet I learned in a very humbling experience that it's not only what you give that is important, but also what you hold back. When I sat with Sidi that afternoon, I realized I had held back a lot—and I didn't want to continue doing that. As he could see all of me anyway, the only person it truly affected was me. I was crippling myself with my withholding.

Sidi was encouraging. He had said that **to be a Sufi is to give up all worries, and there is no worse worry than yourself. When you are occupied with yourself you are separated from God.** If you want to know God, you have to step outside yourself and see that Allah manifests through everyone and everything. It is a big step, and I was a long way from taking that step, because everything was still "all about me."

As I write this, I wonder again if all the things I saved from that first visit are still in storage. When I moved from my big house, I threw out a lot of things I had saved from the period of the breakup of my marriage. I usually recorded every session with whatever counselor Nathalie and I were seeing, and then transcribed each by hand. I had a lot of papers with these writings, as well as the original tapes, but I threw them all away, thinking they had no further use. I had joined all sorts of groups as well, and saved all the notes from those meetings, but then threw them out.

I am tempted to go to the storage unit, and see if I have anything from my first years with Sidi. If there are some things there, they will help me stay closer to what happened and be more truthful. I know I have the notebooks in which I wrote by hand all the teachings; I wonder if I still have the tapes I recorded when he spoke to me, and the notes I made after our meetings.

Yet I don't think it matters that much, because what I want to share is the part I remember, and how it changed my life. I am trying to keep everything as sequential as possible.

I called Maryam in England to ask what she remembered; she said it was too long ago, and she couldn't remember much, but she thought it was a short visit. It was short, but it was also a lifetime. She said she remembered when I came back once with my video cameras and made a film in which she appeared, called *The Truth of a Sufi*—but she couldn't help with much else.

I also called Sidi and asked him, but he said to wait until he next came to the U.S., and we would talk about it. I hope most of this story will be finished by then. What I took from this conversation was: continue, and not to worry.

Later in the evening, Sidi returned once again, and took his place on the mattress on the floor. Dressed in a simple grey jelaba and wearing a knitted kufi on his head, he could have passed unnoticed in the streets of Jerusalem if you knew nothing about him. He was in the world, but not of it, having no apparent connection to the ups and downs the rest of us experience as we struggle with the dunya.

When Sidi spoke about the dunya, it was to say that Allah created it for us to use and to learn from. **The purpose of the dunya was not to use us up, or to make us slaves to material wealth, but to be a lesson in what had value and meaning for us. We had to be sure to keep it in our hands because the dunya could never fill our hearts. "Do not be a slave to the material world," he says. "Let the material world be your slave."**

Sidi told me it was important to realize whom I was serving when I served others, and to know that behind and within everyone I could find Allah's face. I had to be the earth for everyone, especially my children, and should be careful of people who wanted to take everything from me, but not give anything in return. He said I had to be careful with my love, to care about this love, and to look at my beloved sisters in the perfect way.

Keep the door of your love open for everyone who is thirsty for the love of Allah, but in this way, and not in the way of the person; I mean in the perfect way, in the right way.

I pray, from my heart to your heart, to keep you always strong until your wife, Nathalie, can understand, and until she surrenders completely, and she trusts—to be a real beloved for you. From the beginning, when you called me on the telephone, I said to you: "You give her everything, and you open the door for her, but she doesn't see herself in the right way."

Sidi would repeat these thoughts and phrases to me countless times over the next months and years. He put the water of his love on the seeds of my yearning; he nurtured and guided me in the growth I needed to experience, in order to move on to a new life.

Looking back, I don't know why it took me so long. All the things I needed were there: I had the guide; I had the teachings; I had the support team…but I put up such strong resistance. One of my friends said, as he watched me hang on for years to all the pictures I had, "That's the longest bull ride I ever saw."

It would be many years more until Sidi would have permission from Allah to come to the United States. When he did come, I was still not emotionally liberated from all my pictures Nathalie, and of wanting to keep the family together. I cannot over-stress the importance and value of the patience Sidi showed me, and the continual containment he expressed. I still marvel at it all today.

I told Sidi I had read about the tariqa and the meaning of the guide, but was still writing the stations. I said I was ready to surrender to him and bow down to whatever he thought I should do. As I mentioned before, I had followed a lot of diverse paths to get where I was; one of them was an immersion in Hinduism, in which one touched the feet of the guru and, in that way, bowed down to the guru.

(I lost a brother to an accident when I was younger, and it was a major shock to me. It was during a period when I was having a lot of success as a photographer, earning good money and gaining recognition. When my brother died, I went home to see my mom and dad, and I realized there was nothing I could do to help alleviate their pain. Nor did I have the tools to deal with my own. No amount of money could buy a solution. So I returned to Paris, decided to rent my house/studio, took no more jobs, and left for India, where I thought I could find a solution and some guidance. I spent a year there. During that time I met a number of gurus, and learned about kneeling before them and touching their feet.)

Sidi felt strongly about this; he absolutely rejected anyone kneeling before him and touching his feet.

"This is not from our way," he said. **"Prostration is for Allah and not for anything or anyone else. I am nothing without Allah. I am a poor slave and nothing more."**

He said that our way is the complete way, carrying the message of the prophets, and to trust Allah.

Do not throw this message on a stone. Give it to those who are sincere and who seek the light.

Islam carries all the religions, from Adam, Noah, Moses, Abraham, Jesus and all the prophets. To be a real Muslim, you must believe in all the prophets, and to give the truth and to give the love to anyone who wants to know.

When you walk in the world, always be in worship. When we are always in worship, then everything we do is for Allah, and helps us to open the heart so that love can be reborn. Be polite with everyone because everyone is a manifestation of Allah, and be with others as you want them to be with you.

You have a new family now. Love is a closer bond than blood, and the real family for you is with the lovers of

Allah. So be careful and stop keeping company with anyone who doesn't take you closer to Allah.

I did not in any way believe he was telling me to leave my blood family. I felt he was telling me to stop being with people who weren't seeking God, and to spend my time with people who could nourish my heart. I knew I had a tendency to spend a lot of time with people who loved the dunya more than they loved Allah.

Be always with Allah, Salih. There is nothing else. Continue to write the teachings, and be patient. Allah will not leave you. He loves you more than you love yourself. Every pain, every suffering you experience is there to pull you closer to Allah. You have the chance now to sit at the table of Allah and eat the real food. Take your chance, Salih. Take your chance.

And with that he got up to leave. My vessel was obviously full. There was nothing more to say for now. I couldn't even consciously absorb all that he had given me.

How I Fell in Love With the Way

I went back to my room, feeling blessed and encouraged. It didn't last long, but it did inspire me to write for many more hours, though I was exhausted and run down. I didn't want to sleep because I knew I had limited time, and I wanted to get as much of the teachings as I could.

During the day, while out walking with Maryam, I had asked if I could copy some of the teachings on a copy machine, so that I could write them at home. She responded: "Oh no, beloved. The teachings never leave the zawiyah. Sidi does not allow that. You must write the teachings that you want."

"But I don't have time. I have to get back to my children."

"This is Allah's time," she said. "This is your chance, so take your chance and trust Allah." She was sharing the same message Sidi had given me—to take my chance. I did not have to wonder where she got these words.

Years ago I read a book either by or about Jack London, which mentioned a technique he used to stay awake at night in order to write. He tied a string, around his neck, I think; when he nodded off, and his head fell down, it would tug on the string and nudge him awake. I wondered if I could do the same, but I had no string and there was nothing overhead in my room to attach it to. So in my mind I tied a string around my head, and hoped if my head fell it would jar me awake.

I wrote for many hours, finishing the stations of the nafs and the stations of the heart. I paid particular attention to the stations of the heart, because I remembered Sidi telling me I had a pure heart. That statement was to have a long-lasting positive effect on me. Still today, I believe this about myself. I do feel I have a loving heart and, when Sidi told me that, he watered whatever seeds Allah had placed there, and kept those seeds alive so that my heart could grow and expand even more.

Years later, when Sidi was in Santa Fe, many people came to ask him what he saw in them. They asked him to look into their hearts and see where they needed cleaning. They asked how they could deepen their walking and serve Allah more. Sidi saw everything about everyone, and it certainly seemed easier to get him to tell you what was wrong, than to do the work yourself. Well, it was easier to ask; getting him to tell you what was wrong with you was another story.

I was sitting next to him one day, when a rather young couple came before him. They were in their thirties, I think. I knew them—not that well, but enough to know a bit about their story. Actually, I knew the woman. She had come to Sidi a few times, and I was aware of some challenges she was experiencing in her marriage. But I was seeing her husband for the first time.

The woman said that she gave everything to her husband, but he did not love her in a way that nourished her. He only gave her what he wanted, and she was worried the relationship was too one-sided. Sidi looked at her with his heart and his deep eye, and said this was not exactly the truth of what he saw. "He gives you the love in his way, my daughter, and this is a very deep and very beautiful love. He gives you everything you need, but you want the love in your way, and this is why you cannot taste what he has to give you. He is giving you the real love, so surrender to him, and do not try to control him, and you will see Allah through his beautiful heart."

The lady was a bit stunned, but I think something opened in her heart and she saw the truth of Sidi's words. Others had mentioned how lucky she was to have a beloved like she had, and it was too bad she didn't appreciate him more—so when Sidi saw this and told her, I was pretty surprised myself.

After they left, I turned to Sidi and said, "How do you see that, Sidi? You've never met them, but it seems you know everything about them."

Allah shows me.

"I know, but how does He show you? Do you see a picture, or is it words on a page, or a voice?" I wanted to understand how this intuition worked, so I could tap into it to learn more about myself.

It's different every time.

Obviously, this was not something I was ready to hear, or that he had permission to share.

"Well, what do you see when you look at me?" I asked. I wanted to know what nafs was evident in my being, so that I could work on cleaning this state.

As he turned to look at me and the sun sparkled in his eyes, he looked deep into my very being, and said, "Beauty."

I don't share this with you to be boastful, but because it was the single most healing moment I think I've ever experienced. With one word Sidi opened me, and healed me, and helped me believe in myself. I think we all seek approval in one way or another: from parents, peers, loved ones or friends. When Sidi turned his gaze to me, turned his heart to me, and said that single word, it so overshadowed the lifelong criticisms of others that my heart literally melted.

This is how Sidi heals people: He reflects back their own divinity; he does not criticize them or point out negative things about them. He shows them their light, how they are connected to Allah, and how they carry Allah in their own being. He shows them their potential greatness and, with this reflection, gives them a taste of the real love.

In just a moment, he opened that lady's heart to a new dimension of herself and her husband, and taught her that

love is a gift we cannot control—that we must surrender to
our beloved in order to taste the real meaning of that love. In
reality, we are not surrendering to a person, but to Allah, as
Allah comes through that person. As Sidi taught in *The Secret
of the Love of God:* When a person loves the body of a beloved,
they are caught behind a veil. We must go through this veil to
reach the real essence.

I could actually feel inside me the beauty he was seeing; I
could touch it and taste it. It wasn't from me; it was from
Allah. If I was doing anything myself, I was obscuring this
beauty with my nafs. But in that instant, a part of me—
something I had buried and kept hidden—seeped out into a
more prominent place, and planted new seeds of wellness in
my heart. Over the years I have turned my focus inside again
and again, until I can connect with the beauty he made more
clearly manifest. Every time, it becomes easier for me to find
and access what he saw. It's as if he planted a tree that has
since grown; now instead of seeing a seed, I see branches. I
am learning to eat from the fruit of that tree, and find a more
lasting nourishment. And all it took was a second for him to
illuminate that small part of my being.

For this, and the other gifts he has given me and so many
others, I thank him and I thank Allah.

But I was still a long way and many years from that moment
as I sat in the zawiyah, my heart breaking, writing the
teachings and trying not to think about my wife in the arms
of another. I was cooking, as we say, and the fire was pretty

high. Time seemed to go so slowly. I wanted resolution. I wanted my wife to come back and tell me she had a terrible time and was sorry. I wanted her to make me happy again.

I couldn't get my arms around the fact that I had to make myself happy, that I had to love from a place of abundance and from what I had to offer, rather than from a place of need. Looking back at this now, I can see I was truly blessed to have been awakened. Had Nathalie not had the courage to strike out on her own quest, I might never have had the courage to take this path. Because I was so focused on my own pain, I couldn't see the pain and loneliness she must have felt. If she was looking for another man to make her happy, she would run into the same dead end I was at. Our pain does not disappear because someone else gives us love, though it may be reduced, which can throw us off. When the pain of our suffering diminishes beyond a certain point, we no longer feel the immediacy of dealing with it.

Suppose you have a pain in your back. You take a pain killer and the pain goes away, so you don't look anymore for its cause, and you don't go see the doctor. Each time the pain comes back, you take a few pain pills. The pain recedes, and you turn to other, more important things. But then the pain pills cease to work, and you are forced to seek medical attention. The reduction of the pain through the pills might have seemed a blessing but, by the time you get to the doctor, the condition may have worsened. It may be a lot harder to fix than if you had dealt with the cause in the beginning.

This was the way I had been dealing with the immense pain I felt. Maybe there was some pain evident in our relationship before, which Nathalie and I both camouflaged with transient solutions—but now I was in critical care, and no pill was going to help. My life, as much as I wanted it to, did not have an immediate fix. And I would have to find the courage and strength to deal with it. **The only way to reduce this pain would be to open my heart and let the blocked love free. And this wouldn't happen overnight because I was standing in the way—very, very defiant.**

Immediate gratification is an American way of life, and developing patience is not high on the list of priorities this culture teaches. I am not against people who desire to be rich, and quickly. In fact, when it is for the right reason I admire them. Rich means different things to everyone. One can be rich in money, but also rich in love, in family, in skills, and talents and abilities to do things. **The more things or ways you have of being, the more ways you have of expressing Allah's love and message.** Having been blessed with a job I loved, and that paid amazingly well, I didn't often have to wait for things that I wanted. I didn't know how to deal with such an adverse situation, and the trials of patience and surrender, and I wasn't aware that I even had the tools to do so. The beauty, which Sidi later told me he saw, was still hidden from my conscious view, and I was still stuck in many of my pictures. My wife and I were moving in different directions, and a valley was forming between us. I didn't know it at the time, but we would never truly come back together. We tried, more than once, but it just never came to be.

She has a life very different than mine now. Our strongest
bond is the children, and we still connect with each other
through and because of them. I have reached a point where I
feel free of the pain I felt in the past. I have been able to open
my heart and love again, which has been very healing.
Without a doubt, Sidi and the teachings have enabled me to
make this transformation. Sidi says all the time, "Without
Allah, I am nothing." I feel that, without Sidi and the teachings, I am nothing. In a sense, he was not only the doorway,
but the destination. Of course, I say this with the understanding that, because he so carries Allah, Allah is the doorway
and the destination. He is the messenger and the message.

We show our love for Allah by our faith in Him. As our faith
increases, our love increases. And we follow and trust the
guide in the same manner. Once my heart opened and
trusted Sidi, my faith expanded: I felt more drawn to the
prophet, may peace and blessings be upon him, and my commitment to live for Allah was strengthened. Sidi taught me
that one must first follow the acts of the prophet, may peace
and blessings be upon him; then the qualities, then the states.

When I first went to Sidi, I had nothing more than the most
rudimentary understanding of Islam and its messenger. I was
aware of the Koran, had even tried to read it a few times, but
the beauty of its mysteries was hidden from me. I felt no
particular connection to Muhammad, may peace and blessings be upon him, so I had no understanding of his qualities
or states. I did know he was an unlettered man—he could not
read or write—and that the Koran had been revealed to him

while he was in a cave. But that was pretty much the extent of my awareness, and I felt no particularly close attachment.

I thank Allah and Sidi for opening the doorway enough that I could catch even a glimpse of the magnificence of Muhammad, may peace and blessings be upon him. My love for him grows deeper all the time. In my case, being exposed through Sidi to the essence of the messenger of the light, may peace and blessings be upon him, helped create an opening within me that allowed this attraction to develop. Sidi is full of his own love for him; the more one is around Sidi, the more one finds this infectious.

The Muhammad I refer to is so multi-dimensional, so beyond definition, and stands for so much more than I can express in simple words, that I won't try. It is my wish that, through what I write, you will come to understand why I could not, as I wrote it, make this clear. Muhammad is a part of the name of the person who shared these teachings with me, as well as the name of the holy prophet of Islam—and they are both part of an essence of something even greater.

This name carries within it everything that is known to mankind, and I know no words to carry all the meanings or convey all the secrets of this name; I am not yet at a stage of knowing in which I could express all these truths in words. When the bright sun illuminates the heavens, it is difficult to see the stars; they are still there, but their light is hidden within that of the sun. In this same manner, all the light of the prophets who followed the guide of all guides is encompassed by the light of the revelation given to Muhammad, peace and blessings be upon him. His way and his light precede all ways and all light, and his truths encompass all truths. May God grant you and me the power and grace, through His love, mercy and compassion, to taste in even a small way what this name carries.

I have come to see Muhammad, peace and blessings be upon him, as more than the seal of the prophets: He also carries the revelation of Allah. He is an endless, eternal ocean, and his essence permeates all of creation. His name means the praised one, or he who is glorified. When one loves another, describing the worldly picture of that person cannot adequately transmit the depth of feeling. If I were to describe Sidi—his hair color, height and weight, the shape of his head or body—this would in no way describe who he actually is. Nor would it allow you to glimpse the depth or breadth of his spirit. One cannot limit Allah by definitions. No poetry in the world is sublime enough to contain all the feelings of love I have for Sidi or the beloved prophet, may peace and blessings be upon them both.

Sidi has told me that Muhammad, may peace and blessings be upon him, is the father of the heart, and everything and everyone descends from him. Every prophet, every messenger, every guide is his spiritual son. Muhammad is the father of all the prophets in truth and in spirit, but Muhammad is himself the son of Adam in body. Just as all mankind are brothers and sisters, in that we all descend from Adam and are all his children in the body, we are also all children in spirit of Muhammad, may peace and blessings be upon him. The first thing God created, before the rest of existence, was the light of Muhammad.

So I am not so concerned with sharing the facts of the worldly life of the messenger of Allah, may peace and blessings be upon him, as I am with sharing how I came to love what he carries. I do not feel I have the stations of knowing to see the deeper significance of his physical activities. When I watch Sidi, I am simply not aware enough to know the deep meaning behind everything he does and says, but this does not prevent me from opening my heart and loving him. "Do not look at my physical body and expect to know me," he says. So I don't.

We must look with the eye of our deepest longing, with the heart of our greatest himma, if we are to truly approach the guide. Our path to him opens more when our yearning to know him reaches his yearning to know us and take us to the place from which we came. So when Sidi reaches to take your hand, know whose hand you are taking, what is behind it, and what moves it. When you touch his hand, you touch much more than you see with your physical eye. **It is not just the hand of one man; it is the hand of all who have carried the secret, and the truth of the secret. His very movement comes from the depth of Allah's care for His creation. Without this care, his hand could not move.** He is manifested to reflect back our own holiness; his heart invites us to know our own hearts through tasting the love he shares.

In Sidi's teachings, we learn of a moment when Allah took a handful of light from His face and said, "Be Muhammad!" All of creation issued forth from this light, and there is not a prophet who does not find his origin in it. All the spirits of those who love Allah come from this handful of light; if you love Allah and are seeking to know yourself in this way, then you too are from these people. Allah placed this light in us, so that we may use it to find our way back to Him.

All the secrets, truths and sciences have descended through the unfolding generosity of Allah's love through the guide of all guides, the holy bearer of the illustrious Koran, the final prophet, the messenger Muhammad, may peace and blessings be upon him. A beautiful prayer known as Al Wazifa states, "there is nothing that is not dependent on him, and which is not encompassed by his all-pervading secret." And it goes on to say, "Oh Allah! Surely it is Your secret which unites all secrets. And Your light which encompasses all lights. And the guide who leads through You, to You."

With his unlimited and boundless spirit, Muhammad contains the hearts of millions upon millions of those who love him and follow his message, and I have never met anyone who encompasses and exemplifies his holy spirit more than Sidi. When I feel Sidi, I can feel a connection through him to the holy prophet, may peace and blessings be upon them both. I then feel closer to the origin of my creation, which increases my himma and further opens my heart. If you are reading this now, it is because you also yearn to be connected to a spiritual line and know Allah—on this path or another.

When Sidi talks about his own life, I feel that his specialness was obvious from the beginning. When his mother gave birth to him, she was alone in a field. She felt no pain whatsoever. It was an experience unlike any other she'd had. In his early years, Sidi spent a lot of time alone; by the time he was eleven, he could read the Koran and sing it by heart. Those around him, with the eye to see, could see his uniqueness.

Sidi has said there is only one person who knows the complete truth in the world at each moment, although there might be many who know some of the truth. I believe Sidi carries the complete message. For me, this is the difference between a guide and a teacher. There are many teachers; there is only one guide. He has taught me that everything derives from the knowledge of the prophet, may peace and blessings be upon him, and that when he listens to the voice of Allah, it is not with his own ear, just as when he talks, it is not with his own tongue.

The following story is one of the earliest I heard from Sidi about the way his ability to guide and illuminate others was evident from the very beginning.

I want you to do everything with a full heart. Put all your heart into everything you do. I want to tell a very beautiful story that carries deep meaning and gives a true understanding, a deep understanding of trust in Allah and relying on God, and also illustrates a true exchange of love that makes no kind of separation. Even though it is set in two contradictory things, a bird and a wasp, it gives a true understanding of how love and mercy should be expressed. This story teaches us from Allah about deep love and mercy, which every human being aspires to.

This story also shows us that the depths of love go beyond the human being, and are also experienced amongst the other creations of Allah, like his birds and insects.

One day, when I was like thirteen years old, I was in the village that I was born in, and it was harvest time. So they were harvesting the grain and chafing the wheat. I went to see some of my uncles and relatives who were engaged in the harvest time in their village. At one point I turned and saw a wasp, and I saw this wasp go and pick up a grain and fly out. Then I saw the wasp come back and do it again, and then a third time. So I said to myself, there is a story behind what this wasp is doing, and so I decided to catch this wasp without doing it any harm. So I got a very thin thread and a little box. I caught the wasp and tied the thread around one of its legs. And then let it go free. But he came back and picked up another grain and flew away, but I had the thread on his leg and I followed him to where he flew.

After about two hundred yards I saw him flying down and making a sound. Then I found a little nest on the ground. Then I heard the sound of a bird as it was opening its beak. And I saw the wasp go down and drop the grain into the beak of the bird. I took this bird in my hand and I found that this bird had no legs and it was blind. This was a great surprise and it impacted my heart because it was a living class (message), and from that point on I knew that I knew Allah more and more through the interaction of the bird and the wasp.

This was a teaching that I received from Allah through these two creatures. These were my first two teachers because through these two beings, I saw and learned about Allah, because these two creatures had some of the essential attributes of Allah that so few people carry. Only the people who have walked very deeply and have let go of their own selves have achieved this subtlety of being able to carry and transmit these qualities of God.

Because the path is about eventually letting go of everything other than the essentials of Allah. So through what I have witnessed, there I saw the ultimate in love. I said to myself, I will take them and I will charge myself with feeding both of them. But I went first to my grandfather who was a teacher in the mosque. So when I showed him both the wasp and the bird my grandfather started to cry, and the other people were also crying, and they increased in certainty and belief and faith and trust in Allah. And with this my grandfather started to give a teaching on the different meanings that one can understand from this blessed story. He said first we can learn about love, then we can learn about mercy; we can learn about loyalty and, fourth, about trusting in God; and then it is about obliterating all reasons for enmity between all parts of creation.

I saw the ultimate in the deep love that has nothing beyond it. All pictures were annihilated and only the mercy was there to be seen. But look, Allah set up this situation where this bird was being fed by its enemy in the outward. This, for people, is a contradiction. But it is Allah who puts the qualities wherever He wants. He put the qualities of love and mercy in the wasp to feed its enemy, so to speak, and to give it the love. I took the wasp at that point and put it in the little box that I had with me. And I took the bird and put it in another box.

He wants always for you to carry His fragrance, the fragrance of God, because without this fragrance there is no life.

The Gateway to Loving Again

*I*t wasn't until early evening of the next day that I saw Sidi, and by that time my heart and mind were full of questions. I had written a lot more, deep into the stations, and had jotted down many of my questions so that I wouldn't forget them. I was thus fully immersed in the station of the questioning nafs, because most of the questions came from my nafs and were about my wife. There were other questions about the path, and how to walk—but I was predominantly concerned with what was going to happen to my family life.

"What will happen to Nathalie and me, and to our children?"

Sidi's response was simple: "In the end, Allah will make everything good." It now feels as if this has indeed come to be. Of course, at the time, I believed it meant Nathalie would return, and we would live happily ever after.

"How can I open my heart to Allah?"

Although these were my words to Sidi at the time, I have heard them repeated by hundreds of others as they sat with him. A lot of my questions, then and now, are not just my voice asking or my heart seeking. They are repeated by numerous others in one form or another. During the medjlis (when Sidi called to the angels through Maryam), I had asked the same question. The response then had been, "Listen to everything the Shaykh says to you, and follow whatever he tells you to do." The Shaykh's response to me now was:

Open your heart, and see Allah in everyone.

Allah looks at your heart, and if you have sincerity and truth in what you do, and if you are seeking the pleasure of Allah in whatever you are doing and in everything you are doing, then you will find many doors and many secrets will be opened to you. The eyes of the heart see better than the eyes of the head because they see what is deeper, and bring you to see the love that is in everything.

All actions are according to the intentions behind them. If you take a knife to kill a person, this is forbidden. If you take a knife to cut bread, this is permissible. You must use the many gifts of Allah in ways that are beneficial and good for everyone's heart. Use things to feed the spirit in a refined way, in a way that is sacred and this is a prayer. Let these actions with good intentions take you to the presence of Allah.

There is nothing in existence except that it prays and glorifies its lord; all existence sings its song and this is our food and our drink. Animals have hearts and spirits that are more subtle than ours and, if you look with the eye of your heart, you will see that there is love everywhere, and Allah is in every drop of existence.

"When will my wife come back and realize that I am her beloved?"

She needs time until she wakes up to see what God wants from her. This will take time, so you will have to be patient. She is turning many things over in her heart and she cannot see yet a clear way to leave things.

The doors of Allah are open to whoever wishes to enter them. Be like the bee that is always busy and it doesn't go to the rubbish dumps, but to the beautiful flowers. It goes out in the morning and it gives the results of its work to others, because of the love it carries for others.

I know now that I did not do much to help the situation in the next few years, as I was mostly in a reactive and blaming mode. Sidi told me over and over to be gentle, but I was not able to carry and sustain this. I did not know "how to be," so that I could have what I felt I wanted.

"What about my children, Sidi? Will they be alright?"

*Your children will be fine because you give them the real love, and now you have the teachings. Parents need to teach their children the teachings of heaven. **Children need models, not critics.** Today they are too far from the religious teachings, and are taught more about material things. A family cannot do things in front of their children that are contrary to the laws of Allah and expect they would all have integrity. Do not hold on to the material world with so* *much tenacity. Love gives life to everything. It gives you a way of living, and fills you inside with inspiration, and teaches you and the children about right behavior. Care about them from a full heart. Plunge into the arms of your Lord, and you will find that His mercy is greater than that of your own mother when you were a baby.*

Sidi mentioned numerous times—then and over the months and years that followed—that if Nathalie didn't return, Allah would send someone who would be a real beloved, someone who loved Allah very much. As I think about this statement today, I see the truth of it. At that time, I believed he meant another woman; now I think this "someone" has turned out to be me. Allah, through the hand of the guide and the prophet of love himself, may the peace and blessings of Allah be upon them both, has allowed me to rediscover that part of myself. So it is my own self that has been returned to me, and I am now in a place where I can be a real beloved.

I didn't have any conscious idea at the time that, if I could not be a real beloved, I could not receive a real beloved into my life.

We must be who and what we want to have. Sidi teaches that "the understanding of God and all that His love means to you is completed by the sharing of that deep secret love with another." My thought is, this does not only mean another person. It can mean another part of oneself.

"What does Allah want from me, Sidi?"

*To know Him. To carry the message of the peace, and the love and the mercy and the justice. Look with the eye of your heart, Salih, and learn the meaning of love. **Open your heart so you can have everything, but first know the love that is inside you.** Erase everything; leave your past behind and be the son of your moment. Be careful about your holy children, because they are holy jewels, and through their hearts you can see Allah. Care about them and care about the love because, when you care about them, you care about Allah.*

He did tell me I needed to give Nathalie space to find her independence and her own self—and that this would be easier for me "when you come to know yourself, because then you can help her in a deeper way."

I know I didn't understand fully what he was saying. Although my mind grasped it, I would not reach the part of me that could truly comprehend his words until much later. He said that if I could not forgive people's faults, I would never be able to enjoy their virtues.

"The cost of truth can be very expensive," Sidi said. "It is when you give everything to Allah, that He can give everything to you. Don't ask Allah to give you love; ask that He makes you a channel of love."

I asked him about my work, because I felt I could not travel as much as in the past. I had also asked the angels: Their response was that I should look for work that would not take me far away; however, I could continue with photography because I loved it, but not be away for weeks at a time. This response was an indication of all the change that was to come, but I did not see the deep wisdom behind it. Everything I was told clearly indicated that I would be on my own with the kids for quite a while. But the message was delivered with mercy and compassion, so that I would not feel I was being hit by a sledgehammer. Instead, I was offered a message of hope and deliverance. Sidi said:

> *Be patient and do not worry about everything. Be careful about yourself, and about your children, and about your work. Do not think that you are a small star, because you contain everything. Even when you do not see Allah, Allah sees you.*

There was no amount of talking that would allow me to totally understand what I was going through, but it brought me to a point where I was willing to look inside myself, rather than focus on what someone else was or was not doing. I was beginning to grasp that, beyond the world of the senses in which I then lived, existed another world or worlds, which I was getting ripe to explore. Sidi was teaching me that Allah is the protector of all the worlds, both seen and unseen, so I must learn to trust Allah. Sidi teaches that souls not practiced in a life of loving submission cannot bear the intense radiance of paradise.

Unfortunately I was not yet ready to know many things, and truth can only be revealed to those ready to receive it.

Sidi was limited in what he had permission to share with me, because of my low station. There are also probably many things he said to me that I have not held in my conscious memory.

Years later I was to write the following poem, which I would like to share with you now...

WHO IS THE GUIDE

I stand amidst God's grace and beauty
In the dazzling brightness of His light
Looking intently into the shadows of my personality
And feeling trapped in my unsatisfied desires

Demons are dancing in delight
Undulating and tempting
Provocative and proud
Keeping my attention

Using the name as I have been taught, softens those desires
And creates a different kind of longing
But my heart cries, because with this desire
I am filled with sorrow in the longing

Dewdrops sparkle on the leaves
As the light plays upon the field
My Beloved caresses and kisses me with a breeze
That fans the longing even more

How much sweetness does it take
To dispel these demons from my life?
How many kisses on my cheek from my Beloved
To melt the shell around my heart?

I can more than smell the fragrance
I can actually taste it,
But I struggle to sustain it
And the beings in the shadows know of this

With their deceptions
They mask the face of my Beloved,
Tempting me away from my prayers,
Grateful for my ingratitude

And they laugh and make fun of my weaknesses
And the lowliness of my humanity
They take on such pretty faces,
But I have been taught to recognize their subtleties now

And so I look into my heart
Because I know of a force they cannot reckon with
No darkness in the world
Can withstand the ocean of his love

He can drown them in an instant
With a water they cannot resist
I am but a drop in his ocean
And I have drowned in his love more than once

Let them reckon with who he is
And let them try to fool with his sight
Their dances of seduction will be useless
Before the immensity of his patience and compassion

And so I call upon him again
As I have done so many times before
And never has he failed to answer my calling
Mostly I never even need to call

Oh Allah I thank you
And I owe you
And I love you
For sending me my guide

I have learned from Sidi that it is important to occasionally question some of the things we take for granted. When we summon the courage to question these things, we start a different journey. When we head to different places, it helps to feel connected to the guide; this connection increases one's faith, which grows into legs upon which one may walk.

Sidi stayed with me a long time that night. There were many words. There was also silent time during which he said nothing, yet I was not uncomfortable sitting in this silence because I felt so contained—I think it was one of the first feelings of peace I had experienced in a long while. I cannot share everything he said, because some things I have forgotten, some I have no permission to share, and some he simply asked not be repeated.

This was also the first time I got to pray with Sidi. I still knew nothing about the prayer, and could only follow the movements. I felt nervous and was worried that I would make a mistake. The fact that I was behind him eased this nervousness a bit, but I knew he likely had eyes in the back of his head, and there was little he wasn't aware of. The arrogant and prideful part of me that was unable to admit my lack of knowledge was closing down my heart. But my pre-occupation with my current situation still overwhelmed any other desire, so I continued to ask questions I thought might help me live with the pain.

If I could have trusted more—if I had thrown myself into the prayers and learned all I could about how to pray and what it all meant—I might have had answers that could have shortened my time of pain, and taken me to a better place much more quickly. But we each have our own path and our own destiny, and I suppose I was fated to live mine the way I did.

So I continued relentlessly along the same lines and, as always, Sidi held me with his heart and his infinite patience.

*Don't worry about anything that meets you because He is with you, and He helps you, and all that He wants is for you to continue walking, and with the deep patience. **In any case, thank Him about what He gives.** But this doesn't mean to stop with the old pictures from your life with this woman who has broken the cup of your love, and who has left your garden. God gives her a deep chance to fix everything and to return to you, and to live with each other,*

and to build a new home. But this house, it is very
important for it to be like a holy mosque where you can feed
yourself, and she also, if she likes.

Looking back, it seems obvious what Sidi was telling me, but
I could not assimilate it in a positive way at the time. It
would take a long time until I could "thank Him about what
He gives." I have heard Sidi say this to countless others who
have met with the same challenge I encountered around this
teaching. **Thanks is best given before supplication, because
it opens one's heart. Giving opens us to receiving.**

When one is in the fire, it is not easy to follow this advice and
"thank Allah" for what is happening. When one reaches this
moment, true change can happen—but I took so long to get
there. Yet it makes sense if you think about it: **Why would
Allah give you more, when you are not grateful for what
you have? How sincere can you be in asking for more, if
you are not happy with what you have already been given?**

We all have countless gifts for which we are not consciously
grateful. Life and the ability to breathe, food on the table, a
bed to sleep in, the ability to lift one's finger, and the ability
to think and feel, are but a few. No matter how pained our
hearts, we can be thankful to have a heart that can feel. All
this is much easier said than done because, while suffering a
deep pain (physical, emotion or spiritual), it is not easy to
thank Allah. But over and over again, I have heard Sidi say, "I
thank Allah."

In his teachings, Sidi says repeatedly that, when we came into this dunya, we came with nothing. Allah fed us as babies with deep care; He feeds us always because He cares about us. He loves us. He wants to teach us to live only for Him, but this is a deep walking for many. We must learn to trust him deeply in order for this surrender to happen.

I was not in the deep trusting. Allah, in His infinite mercy and compassion, had led me to the well to drink—but I was sitting there thirsty, sipping, when I should have been gulping. I was nibbling, when I should have been eating. And I did not hear with my deep ear all that he was telling me. I did not respond to Sidi's instructions to make "the real tawba," (repentance), and to learn "how to take and how to give."

One starts what Sidi calls "the real tawba" by surrendering to the guide. He can share with us all that is in the holy books; he is the channel through which we can access the light and love that contain the truth. Once we surrender to him, once we take the promise, the covenant of Allah, we are considered to be real beloveds—and we can start our walking in a more sincere way.

I was ready for this. Whether because I was so lost and desperate, or because the pain was so strong, or because Allah's calling was so great…something in my heart, and for this I thank Allah, was ready to let go and surrender to Sidi. **I could not feel the subtle presence of Allah, as much as I sensed the powerful connection Sidi had with Allah. He** was the bridge to the place I wanted to go and, though that place was far away and I could not see it on the horizon, the bridge was tangible; it was there for me to walk upon. I knew it could lead me where I wanted to go—even if I wasn't sure where that was, because I couldn't describe with awareness the destination I sought.

When Sidi left that night, to return to his family and to the place where he slept, I went back to the little room that had become my home, my place of refuge—a place that felt like the only security I could identify at that time.

I sat on the bed, on the floor, for a long time. I took notes about what Sidi had said. And I wondered about my next step. I hadn't finished writing the stations; I knew I wanted to complete that task as quickly as possible, but couldn't stop wondering about which to do next. I wanted to write them all, but knew I could not. So instead of appreciating what I had and thanking Allah, I went again to that place of fear and lack and wanting.

When I recognized that I was doing this, it opened an even more immense sadness in my heart. In little time, I was weeping from a deep place. This time there was no Sidi, no Maryam to come and comfort me. And though I know now that Sidi's spirit was right there with me, I was heading to the most private place inside my heart that I had ever been. I don't know how much time it took. Looking back, I think that each day I was there, I went to a deeper place. **I do know that, by the time I was ready to leave, I had touched a place**

inside my being that absolutely knew this was my path, Sidi was my guide, and the divine presence I sought was not just in this holy city of Jerusalem, but in the places Sidi helped me find within my heart.

Many months later—in fact, it might have been many years—I had an experience born from that moment, from that visit to Jerusalem and the private place Sidi helped me access. Even when I returned to Santa Fe, and the magic of my proximity to Sidi had worn off a bit, I continued to work intimately with him. There was a single instant, maybe the biggest shift I experienced, which I want to share with you now.

When I got back to Santa Fe, I reverted back to a lot of my old ways. When I didn't sense a shift in Nathalie, when she told me how much she was attracted to the man she had gone to visit, I was once again overcome with fear of loss, and unable to contain her in a positive way. She ended up moving out of the house, getting her own place, and living a life that seemed free of my constant criticism and accusations. In truth, however, she was never free; we had contact because of the kids, and I would shame her as much as possible at every opportunity.

For years, every day seemed an eternity, and I struggled to make it through each one. I was unhappy and ungrateful, and my heart was closed. I was convinced that, to be happy again, I would have to have the love come through the face of Nathalie, and there was simply no other solution. There were so many people that reached out to help me, so many that sent love and support—but instead of drinking from their hearts, all I thought about was Nathalie. When would she give up the others and come back?

My four children were deeply affected by my sadness. Carl Jung once said, "Nothing so affects the life of a child as a parent's unfulfilled life"—and I was not a good example of a happy and fulfilled parent. The younger kids were insecure about me leaving for even short periods of time; for years they both slept in my bedroom, one in the bed with me, and one on the floor beside the bed.

When I returned home from running errands in town for an hour, they would always rush to greet me as if I had been away for a month. I think that, although they were tolerant of my relationship with Sidi, they didn't quite know what to make of me, my connection with Islam, my praying in a way they had never seen, and the other changes they sensed since my visit to Jerusalem.

I still had trouble sleeping, so I was tired all the time. That broken sleep pattern still affects me today. Before everything happened with Nathalie, I slept well. My head would hit the pillow and I would fall asleep immediately—but now I sleep in an irregular pattern, which is not necessarily healthy for me, because I feel tired a lot.

Whether the sun was shining or the day was cold and rainy, I was only aware of an immense sadness in my heart. I continued to complain to anyone with the patience to listen, including my children. Nura mentioned that she didn't feel I should do this, that it wasn't healthy, as they were not ready to contain this kind of information. I maintained they could feel it anyway—and my parents had hidden so much from me about their feelings that I thought, once you grew up and made a certain income, problems didn't exist anymore. For me, the reality of being a grown up was that you got a job, married, and lived happily ever after. In the society I grew up in, people were more than discreet about their private lives and pain, and were intent on "keeping up with the Joneses," as this lifestyle became known. People did not show their weaknesses, and everyone put on a good face at all times. The consequence for me was that I had no skills to deal with all that happened when the walls came crumbling down.

One day, when I returned from running errands in town, Justin and Tara (my two youngest children) came running down from the dining area, shouting "Daddy!" with so much happiness to see me, so much love in their hearts, that something quite magical happened. I don't think they had greeted me any differently all the other times I had come home, but this time something in me opened. As I lifted Tara, the smallest one, and as Justin grabbed me around the waist— for the first time since the walls had crumbled I felt about ten seconds of actual bliss. I could feel their love for me but, more importantly, I felt something positive flowing from me.

Later that night, as I lay in bed and reflected on this moment, I came to realize what had happened for those ten seconds: I had opened my heart, and allowed myself to love again. For all the years my heart had been shut down, no gratitude flowed from me, no love flowed from my heart. Sidi's words came back to me: **"Open your heart; thank Allah about what He gives; give the love that you want to receive..."** I got out of bed and started to wander around. I went to the living room, sat on one of the bancos and looked around. I had a special house—a paradise, in fact—that all the kids adored. I could put food on the table. We all had good health. I realized how lucky I was. This was clearly a defining moment in my life.

I went back to my bedroom and stood over the sleeping little ones. My heart opened, and love poured from me to them— love that had been blocked for so many years. I thought about Justin and Tara, and how much they depended on me to fill the vacuum created when their Mom left. I looked at their faces and their hearts, and tears came to my eyes.

I went into the older kids' bedrooms and stood over them. I marveled at the magic and magnificence of who they were. I knelt down by their beds and kissed their faces. I thought about all the magic I had experienced when Jessica, my first daughter, was born, and the immense feeling of love that awakened in my heart through her. I thought about her riding her horses and doing all the things she loved, about her honesty and integrity. I thought about all the moments I had shared with my son Jason, all the hours we had spent on the tennis court together, how he made me laugh—how he was so like me.

During this time, I gained a deep understanding of what had happened in those earlier ten seconds of happiness, and the feeling came back, stronger and more powerful. I felt another ten seconds of happiness, and then another. Then the ten seconds became a minute, and I knew I had discovered something inside of me that would be my path back, something tangible that I could touch and access at will. All the pain I had felt was the love that was blocked. I didn't need Nathalie to love me in order to feel happiness. **What a revelation this was! All I needed to do was to open my heart, thank Allah and give the love.**

I went back to my bedroom and knelt down next to our dog, Calinou. A calin in French is a cuddle, so his name meant "little cuddle"—but I gave him a big cuddle, and it felt good. I wanted to wake the kids and share my heart with them but, instead, I let them sleep and opened my heart more and more to them. I walked to my office, and looked around. I sat in the chair at my desk and thanked Allah for having always sent some financial miracle to sustain my family over the years. (I was still spending more every month than I took in, but we had survived.)

And I thought about Sidi.

I thought about all he had told me, and why I hadn't been able to practice what he had said. I thought about how stupid I had been, and wondered why it took so long to finally wake up. I thought about Nura and Tarik, who had been so supportive, and how I must have driven them nuts with my constant complaints. I thought about my parents and sisters, and how I had not always been present with them.

I continued to walk around the house. At my desk, I stopped in front of a photo of Sidi, which I had taken in Jerusalem. I don't know if I wanted to cry, or scream for joy. I looked out the window, and saw the beauty of nature…the moon shone brightly and illuminated the New Mexico landscape. To this day, I don't know why it took so many years to wake up to that moment. It now seems so obvious: If I had just listened to Sidi and done what he said, I could have been free of the pain so much more quickly. Maybe all those years were necessary—maybe, I thought hopefully, the tawba was more complete this way.

Since that moment I have tried to share the truth I experienced on that special day with others I have felt were "stuck" in the same station I was then. When I meet someone in pain, I tell them of my experience—that I thought my pain came from what I wasn't getting but, in truth, it came from what I wasn't giving. Yet I have not once felt that they were any more ready to hear it than I was, when Sidi explained the way out of my pain and, in reality, drew the map. I guess we all have to wait for our moment. Then, when the time is right, and with Allah's grace, we can move from where we are stuck, to where we want to be.

There is hadith that I like: The Messenger of Allah, peace and blessings be upon him, said:

The people most severely tested are the prophets; then the righteous; then the next best and the next best. A man will be tested in accordance with the degree of his religious commitment; the stronger his religious commitment, the stronger his test.

I think I was committed, deep in my heart, to Islam, but it took a long time to surrender to this commitment. Allah's grace and Sidi's commitment to guiding me sustained my yearning, until the sparks of this yearning could be fanned into a fuller flame.

As I grew more comfortable practicing gratitude, many things changed in my life. One of the big things, which finally released me from the attachment I felt to Nathalie, was the ability to open my heart to her in a new way. One day— I don't remember exactly when it was—I decided I was destroying myself with the anger I felt toward her, and that it was an incapacitating and destructive force in my life. So I took a pen and paper, and started making a list of all the things I was grateful to her for. At the top of the list, of course, was our four children. I went into my heart and relived the birth of each child. As I returned to these moments, my heart opened in a huge way. I felt immense love toward her for all she had gone through in carrying each child, and the pain of childbirth. I thought about the closeness we had felt in the actual moments of making love, when our babies were conceived. And, for the first time in what had seemed like an eternity, my heart felt warm and loving toward her. Even today, when we have a disagreement about one of the children, I choose to remember these moments and focus there, rather than on something negative.

I suggest strongly that anyone reading this try this process until you feel its power. **If the love you feel toward someone is blocked, find the place inside you where it once lived. Because love is eternal, and cannot die, you will find a place in your heart where it exists. And as Sidi would say: "Give thanks to Allah, today and not tomorrow. Be the son or daughter of your moment, and take your chance now."**

In the years since this teaching came into my heart, I have found I use it all the time. If something is not going well in my business, I go to find where the love is blocked, where I am unhappy or not in a joyful state. Then I look for a way to open my heart and let the love flow again.

After the breakup with Nathalie was final, and we were divorced, I had some challenges in my work. Since most of the kids had grown older and left the house, I decided to sell the place where we had all lived together. Tara, my youngest daughter, was still living with me; she was around 15 when I sold the house. I think she is still sad, even a bit angry, that I sold it; I think she still misses it, but I believe in my heart that one day she will know it was a good thing to move on.

When we moved, I had trouble finding someone in town who would rent to me: A lot of places didn't allow pets, and we still had Calinou. So when Tara and I moved, it was to a rather unattractive house, and it was not an easy thing for either of us. Suddenly, we were cramped up in a tiny place, instead of the large and roomy house we had lived in. It was a particularly sad and painful experience for Tara, and a deep emotional shock for her.

I had entered into another relationship, with a woman named Gina, and thought that moving into town (and closer to her) would help. I was not ready to commit to anyone; my life was still pretty much a mess in many ways—especially financially—but we both thought living closer would help. I spent a lot of time over the next couple of years feeling a bit down and sorry for myself, worrying about money and about Tara. I had not yet assimilated a feeling of gratitude in enough areas of my life. I accepted my situation, but I could hardly say I felt *grateful*.

However, when I finally did find more than just acceptance in my heart—when I found a true and authentic feeling of thankfulness—my financial situation improved, as did my living situation. I reached a point when, after years of Sidi telling me to trust Allah, I actually did start to trust Him. With this trust came a true, deep sense of satisfaction with my life and with myself. But more of this later…

As far as this story is concerned, I am still back in Jerusalem, it is still early in the visit, and I still have a lot to learn. Some of the seeds that Sidi planted in my being during that visit have still not sprouted into anything tangible or visible. It was going to take a lot of patience on his part—and surrender on mine—until I would find the fruit of these plants.

Being the Son of My Moment

I spent a lonely time that evening. I felt so isolated. I was deeply concerned that, when I sat and repeated the name as Sidi had told me to do, I didn't feel the ecstasy the teachings described. Maybe everyone has stations they get stuck in, which others will breeze right through. When I prayed, I was more concerned with what I was doing wrong than with experiencing the peace and benefits of the prayers. Yet I do love Allah, and think of Him all the time. When things are going well, my whole life can feel like a prayer, so I must force myself to stay disciplined and not miss the actual prayers. I know many people who truly seem to love prayer times; they look forward to these moments and feel fulfilled.

In the last years, learning Arabic, learning to write the Fatihah (the prayer that is recited five times a day) in Arabic, and working on better pronunciation have all deepened my understanding and furthered my sense of appreciation. One thing that always appealed to me about Islam is that, instead of setting aside one day for worship, as I was taught to do as a Christian, prayer is woven right into the fabric of daily life.

As Sidi mentions again and again in his teachings, "we should strive for constant remembrance and gratitude. These principles become grounded in our existence through constant practice and repetition. To be absent from your Lord is a great sin."

When we open our hearts, we are introduced to a new language: the language of the soul. I was starting to sense this, and could feel parts of myself that I had long neglected finally being addressed. A friend of mine who is a shaman once told me that, as people grow up in American society, many rituals and rites of passage are ignored. When we pass into adulthood without completing these rituals, there are holes in our personalities—incomplete parts of us—that throw us out of balance. He said parts of my manhood were incomplete, and I needed to look at and deal with these areas.

I think there is truth in this, and I felt that Sidi was working with these undeveloped parts in a deep and profound way. For example: I had a lot of unresolved issues around my father, especially ones of acceptance. Having Sidi in my life has helped me feel more complete around this. Even though we are not far apart in material years, his love is eternal and his wisdom is ancient. So he fulfills the father's place in my life, and I feel complete in that area now. Sidi teaches that there are ties stronger than blood, and I have felt the truth of it. In one of Sidi's books, *The Path to Allah Most High*, he mentions this:

> *To save the self nowadays is an individual duty. This duty includes repentance, patience, perseverance, gratitude, hope, fear, humbleness, asceticism, longing, cordiality, satisfaction, short duration of hope, and love of death. Since this knowledge is an individual duty, its seekers should travel to its source even if they have to disobey their parents.*

I mention this because I would have to disobey my parents, with respect to all the pictures I had around family and the way things should be done. I was brought up to believe a lot of things my parents were taught to believe and, as they did not question as much as I did, they still believed these principles worked. To find my way out of my pain, I would have to listen to the guide—not to my nafs, or to other people of the material world.

People repeat what they're taught to repeat as solutions to how to live; but I've found that, as Sidi says, it is best to follow your heart rather than your mind. I have never lived in fear of rules, so disobeying others' ideas was not a particular challenge to me. But I know that for some, this is extremely difficult.

Sidi teaches that the best path to knowledge is through an increase in acts of obedience, rather than through our senses, because the knowledge that comes through our senses can be deceptive. At that time, my senses dictated my life, because I was reacting to so many things. I was more obedient to my senses than to acts of obedience toward Allah. Sidi writes in *The Path to Allah Most High:*

> *The knowing of everything comes through Allah, and this knowledge is not blemished by doubts and confusion and ignorance. Allah has made knowledge of yourself a means for your knowledge of Him. The divine overflowing is vast, and your share is only what you can receive of it from your self.*

So even though I was in Jerusalem, by his side, I could only take what I was able to at the time. There were no limits to where Sidi could guide me, except those I imposed. Because so many parts of me were separated from each other during that time, I could feel no unity within myself. Until I resolved some of these things internally, I saw that nothing else could be resolved. It would take time for me to integrate enough of my internal conflicts so that I could feel an overall peace.

Sidi told me what to do; he offered the keys, but I was simply unable to cross through my fears and grasp the hand he extended. I saw the physical hand, but had a limited view of what was behind it. **I could touch the heart that was containing me, but couldn't experience the true vastness and infinite richness of that heart, which contained so much of which I was unaware.** He told me so many times:

> *Walk, and continue to walk. Then you see through the remembering of the Name of Allah the real help, and through the teachings that you have.*

> *When Allah is called upon by any of His names, He answers according to the meaning of the name. The prophets always kept the adab (politeness) with Allah, because they knew that they came short of understanding what is the Self of Allah.*

Well, if the prophets fell short, it's not hard for me to accept that my station is certainly far from theirs. I cannot over-emphasize the importance of having—in tangible form,

in front of me—a physical manifestation of divine presence
with whom I could interact and relate. I could imagine a
world of Abraham and Moses and Jesus—but to sit face to
face with Sidi and actually touch that reality made a huge
difference for me. I can still experience the kaleidoscope of
beings I saw when I met Sidi the first night in the zawiyah; I
have seen him, when he speaks of the prophets, reflect their
qualities back to countless beloveds.

Often, when we all sit together, someone will ask a question
about one of the prophets, and I can actually feel the presence
of this prophet as Sidi brings him into his heart. I am not
alone in this; many beloveds have shared with me that
they've had a similar experience. Sidi says:

*I offer what I have been commanded to offer: a message of
truth and unity and guidance in the way of Allah. We make
no separation between any of the messengers; we make our
actions for the sake of Allah and our end satisfaction is in
His pleasure. And we ask Him to grant us His love and His
mercy and His peace.*

*Allah is the revealer of secret divine knowledge. When hate,
envy and jealousy disappear, illness goes away. Destroy
your humanity and rise to the divine, spiritual world. As
levels increase, so does transparency. Read, understand and
believe, and be reborn. The divine human gives birth with
each instant. Heal your soul and then your body can heal.
The secret is in the love. If you know Allah, you will be
great and you will heal. Only Allah remains and you*

remain in Him when you are a believer. Allah is your protector, We are from the light of our Lord, so it is natural for us to be polite. Do not be forgetful for even one instant in your remembering of your lord. Deal well with the divine world and it will deal well with you.

We are created from a single source and we should not corrupt it by corrupting ourselves. Let the seeds stay pure and blossom into compassion, mercy and divine understanding. Don't stop with understanding but apply it. By following the practices you will become more pure, and with the purity your hand becomes divine and you can heal others as well. This way is an ocean with no shores, and you are a small fish swimming in that vast ocean. Follow the natural system of Allah's teachings because walking properly fills your heart. Have nothing in your heart other than the love of Allah. Make the journey a divine one. You carry the mirror of divine reality. Return to the original image of pure light and the divine Adam. Adam in the ancient language means dust. Vanish in Allah and walk in the divine realm, and there you will see there is no disease. There is limitless generosity with no boundaries. Be the tongue of divine politeness. Be humble.

We are taught to follow the guide, and use the disciplines and follow the teachings in order to cleanse ourselves. **When our himma, our yearning for Allah, fills us enough that we are drawn to meeting Sidi—and thus are willing to open our hearts and surrender—then our desire to know Allah meets Sidi's desire to lead us to Allah. In the meeting of these two**

passions, a new creation is brought forth. Sidi is the spiritual father of this new creation, and he knows how to nurture and water the seeds so they can blossom into a fuller expression.

Our purpose in life is to know Allah, and one of Sidi's purposes is to bring us to this knowing. He has the ability to show us everything we need to know about our selves by mirroring back to us any part of our selves that needs to worked on. He can see into subtle parts of our beings that are still veiled from our own gaze; he can start working on these by stimulating processes that need to be initiated. The beloveds are so important to Sidi because, if there were none for Sidi to guide, it would be like throwing seeds upon a rock, rather than into the fertile hearts of the seekers. When you plant seeds in your garden, hoping for a spring crop, some will grow and others won't—even if you water them all the same.

I have always been in a rush to do things, and wanted to go as fast as possible. But I've learned that the ant and turtle know more about the road than the animals that speed across it. So I've started to slow down and learn to absorb things more. I'm learning to appreciate the voyage, and not worry so much about the destination. Some seeds take longer to grow than others, so I've decided to spend more time "watering the garden."

I think people often feel that, once they find religion or discover a path that might lead them to God, life becomes easier.

They feel there will be no further serious challenges. **I learned that when Allah, in His mercy and compassion, brought me face to face with the guide, the real challenges could begin—because now I was equipped to deal with everything.** I can't imagine facing some of the things I've faced in the last years without Sidi there to guide me. I never thought any part of me could be grateful for the pain that brought me to Sidi, but I do have to wonder if I would have gotten there without it. Maybe it was in my destiny, but I had to go through a certain door to get to that destiny. God offers us thousands of possibilities every moment, which we don't always take—sometimes because we don't see them, sometimes because we are scared. There are as many reasons as opportunities, and our nafs is always there, saying to do or not to do. Fortunately, through following the guide and his teachings, we can develop the parts of us that need to trust, and learn which inner voices to listen to.

It is like a second birth when one meets the guide. And the child that one was must leave the past and accept the new creation. Forgetting the past is a form of freedom that can liberate you, and create a space within you to receive the deep blessings Sidi carries. **The ancient truths of which he speaks come from an unbroken line of prophets and messengers. When we open our hearts and surrender to him, we open ourselves to this direct connection.**

Our parents don't always understand this and, as I have pointed out, Sidi addresses this. He states in *Music of the Soul*:

*Then your family comes to you and they tell you to live in
their way. This is also from the face of the shaitan, yet this
should make the student more determined to leave
everything, because you know that this is the right way,
you cannot listen to anything else.*

I had a powerful experience with Sidi concerning my father,
which I would like to share with you.

I was in Santa Fe and had some clients in town, because I was
working as a photographer. My Mom called to say my Dad
was in the hospital; he was not doing well, and she thought I
should come to see him. This was about the third or fourth
time she had said things to get me to visit, so I wasn't sure I
trusted her, or that things were as bad as she said. I knew she
loved the visits, especially when I brought the kids, so I never
thought badly of her doing this. It just made it a bit difficult
to believe her all the time.

She had been sick herself, with a rare blood disease; she was
one of few people who did not die from it. At this time, my
Dad took care of her. He was retired and had little focus in
his life outside of her care. When she got well, he got sick.

I had never been particularly close to my Dad. In fact, he had
adopted me, and had a hard time accepting my rebellious
behavior and habit of living outside the traditions he had
been brought up to believe in. He had gone to private
schools, then Yale; then he went into the family business. I
had gone to private schools, been kicked out of one, been to

Yale and dropped out, and never got close to going into the family business. He had two children of his own with my Mom, and they were closer to him in many ways.

However when he lost one of those children, his son, to an accident, he was devastated and in great pain. During that time we actually drew near to each other. I think he started to appreciate my spiritual searching, even though it had turned away from the traditional Christian church with which he was comfortable. At one point, he even said to me, "I might have lost one son, but I feel as if I've gained another." It was the warmest and most loving moment I can remember with him. (So now you can see how important it was for me to have the healing of a father relationship with Sidi.)

Looking back, I realize my Dad did for me what he believed was right. Maybe his love wasn't always perfect, but the intent of his love was pure. He put up with an amazing amount of resistance and foolishness from me, and I think a lot about that now—especially with four kids myself. My kids have given me little grief in my life, and I am blessed for that. Once, after listening to a song called *In the Living Years* by Mike and the Mechanics, I wrote a long and loving letter to my Dad that shared my gratitude for all he had done for me, for my brothers and sisters, and for my Mom. If you have living parents, I strongly urge you to share your love now, before it is too late and they are gone.

So here I was, with clients in town, extremely busy, and not feeling strongly that I should rush off to New York. I happened to call Sidi with some questions about the non-profit I run for him and, in the course of this conversation, mentioned my mother's call.

This is right, my son. You should go.

"When should I go?" I asked.

Soon.

"Well I have people in town Sidi, and work. Will it be alright if I go this weekend?" (It was a Monday.)

No, you should go sooner than that.

"What do you mean by sooner Sidi? Like Thursday or Friday?"

No, sooner than that.

"Should I try to get a ticket for tomorrow, Sidi?"

Today would be better.

It was already about 11 am. I got nervous, and told him I was now worried whether my Dad was alright.

Sidi assured me that all was well—but that I should be the son of my moment and go. I called the airport and found a 1 pm flight. However, since I lived an hour from the airport, I had to leave in the next few minutes. I quickly called my clients, explained the situation, gave them a number for another photographer, and said I had to go. They told me not to worry. We had not started the actual photos yet, so this was not a major problem. They would relax for a few days and search locations.

I got to the airplane literally as they were shutting the door, and arrived in the hospital in the evening to see my Dad. I was stunned to see how bad he was, and how weak. Because it was late by the time I got there, I didn't get to spend much time with him. He was pretty out of it anyway. But I wondered about the power of Sidi, and how he had seen how bad my Dad was all the way from Jerusalem. He had never even met him; neither had I talked a lot about him. I went home with my Mom, and returned the next morning.

And I got another shock. There was my Dad, sitting up in bed, eating breakfast as if nothing was wrong. He seemed genuinely happy to see me, especially since I had made the effort to fly from Santa Fe. We talked for about half an hour. Then he was taken away for some tests, and I went to a pay phone and called Sidi.

"As-Salaam Alaykum Sidi. This is Salih. I'm with my Dad in New Jersey, and you were right to tell me to come. Last night when I got here he wasn't doing well at all, but today he seems so much better."

This is the mercy of your visit, beloved.

"Well, do you think I should go back now to Santa Fe to finish that job?"

Not now. Wait a little longer.

I spent most of the day with my Dad; early in the afternoon he started to slip away. I read to him from the Bible, and we talked of many things. At one point he looked me straight in the eyes and said, "I love you." It was the only time in my whole life I remember him saying that.

Little by little, he slipped away, with the same dignity and simple elegance with which he had lived. I still marvel today at the depth of seeing that Sidi showed me that day, and I realize that without his guidance and love, I would have missed one of the most tender and beautiful moments in my life. **I was so proud of my Dad, how he lived in those last moments, and how he modeled to me things he had probably shown me his whole life but I was too shallow to acknowledge. I know now that his heart and mine are one, and the only real differences were things of the dunya, which matter little.**

It is said that "the path of the folk is effacement." My Dad seemed to have reached that station at the end. I am so glad I was able to trust Sidi, and do what he said without question. This incident has certainly deepened my walking with him.

My Dad tried to pass on to the children the values that he learned from his family. His parents both had strong personalities, and I know he wanted to please them. He never seemed to have met anyone whom he respected that challenged him on these beliefs, so he pretty much followed the same path all his life. My Mom was quite creative, and thought a lot more outside the box than he did. But he seemed to worship her: He did marry a divorced woman with children, which was a pretty adventurous thing to do. I imagine his parents were not too pleased with the idea, but he went forward with it anyway.

The idea of "keeping up with the Joneses" was prevalent as I grew up, and both my parents lived in that world. It was important that the outside picture of people's lives look good, and many went deep into debt to look good on the outside.

Somehow, when I got into my late teens, I started meeting people from outside that world; I made friends with artists, singers, actors—people that came from a completely different world. I started experimenting with smoking grass—which replaced the drinking I had done in the world I grew up in— and I started to meet people who lived a much freer and, to me, more attractive lifestyle. So leaving my parents to find my path was not a problem for me. In fact, I think it was my salvation. I was not made to live a life conforming to other people's thoughts.

There is tremendous freedom to be found when one is able to leave the past behind and be the son of his moment. At one point in my life I went to live in Paris, where no one knew anything about me. When people know nothing of you, there is no anticipation of how you will react or be in a certain situation, so you can become a whole new person.

Sidi remakes himself all the time, which makes him unpredictable in many ways. He lives in the moment and, because he lives in so many worlds, that moment is huge. So when you're with him, you are actually with just a small part of him—but he is with all of you, because we are like open books to the eye of his heart.

When I returned home to Santa Fe after my first visit to Jerusalem, I was like a new person. But I wanted my children to feel comfortable with me, so I gradually introduced the new parts of myself. The love I felt for them was much deeper because my heart had opened more; I followed Sidi's teaching that speaks of always giving to the hearts of others what we would wish our own hearts to receive, were our circumstances reversed.

Because of what Sidi taught me, I have always encouraged my children to follow their hearts—to be who they want to be, not who others might like them to be. They all know well the importance of God in my life, but I have never forced them to be like me or think like me. I watch Sidi with his blood children and with all his other children (the beloveds). **I see the freedom he gives everyone, and it makes me think this is how Allah is with us. He loves us unconditionally, and His love is always there. His heart is always open, to receive us as fully as we want to plunge into it.** As I watch how Sidi's family takes care of him and loves him, I strive to be like this with my Mom. Sidi has said he finds it ludicrous that we set one day aside for "mother's day" in this culture because, for him, mother's day is every day.

Allah says: "All in creation are the children of God, and the most beloved to God are those who are the most useful, most generous, to the children of God." So we are taught to give the love, openly and freely, and be like the candle that consumes itself to give light.

Get rid of the parts of your personality that prevent you from opening your heart and letting your light shine. Then you can carry the message of the love and the peace and the mercy and the justice. As Sidi says:

> *People need the love. Carry out loud these teachings because they will lead you and others to the true knowing of God, and illuminate not only others' way, but your own as well.*

Persevering in Patience

I don't remember a lot of specifics about the next day, my third in Jerusalem. I do know I had very little sleep, and spent most of the night writing the teachings. I was preoccupied, trying to find a way to bring some of the papers back with me to the U.S. I wanted to continue copying them but, more than anything, I wanted other people to read them. As I wrote the teachings, there were many moments in which my heart felt compelled to share these ideas—first with my children and Nathalie, but also with others I knew would love to taste what I was experiencing.

One memory I still carry from those days is the breakfast Maryam made for me in the morning. It was simple: eggs, tomatoes, hummus, and pita bread with an herb called zatar. I remember sitting with her at the kitchen table. As we shared the food, and a delicious tea she had made, she had a shawl wrapped around her to protect against the cold. At that time, it tasted like one of the most exquisite meals I'd ever had. There was something magical in the experience: the unique sounds of the Middle East floating through the window; the uniqueness of the landscape; the image of Maryam, wrapped in her shawl; the odor of the meal. All combined to produce something special in my heart.

I was surprised that something so common as a breakfast created this sensation. I've been fortunate in many ways in my life. I've traveled widely and eaten breakfast in some beautiful places with many special people, including presidents, rock stars, famous actors and multi-millionaires—and my kids, who are the most special. Yet none of those meals ever felt as special as the breakfast I had that morning with Maryam. **I felt this was the real food Sidi referred to, that it wasn't only the material food on the table, but everything else with which I was being nourished.**

It was an early lesson to me that, when we pay attention to everything, we are able to absorb and experience much, much more. I see now that many of the things I valued and thought important before have changed significantly.

All that day, I was conscious of how much Sidi's teachings point out the sacred aspects of life, so when he returned in the evening I asked him how to be in the world, and how to see Allah in everything. He said:

> *Don't get caught in the material picture. We are giving a spiritual food as well as food for the stomachs. This gives strength and sustenance for the people to walk on this path.*

So I was being fed in ways to which I was not accustomed, though I don't think I was especially conscious of it at the time. But I knew it felt different, so I started asking Maryam how she had made the things, thinking the specialness was actually in the material food, unaware that it lay in what was behind everything.

So when you are in Sidi's physical presence, I encourage you to not make the same mistakes I did, by focusing on the outside picture...look deep in your heart, see what is inside everything, and look for a deeper significance. If he serves you a bowl of rice and lentils, as he is known to do, know that, when you eat this food, you are eating a lot more than you see on the plate. **There is a special kind of love in this food, as well as humility, a passion to serve and care for others, a commitment to nourish and sustain, a willingness to give; there is mercy, compassion, an example of how to be with others, of how not to think you are better than someone else. It is a chance to witness what he means when he tells the story of caring for everyone's shoes.**

When a painter looks at a painting, he has a different perspective than I might. He looks at the technique, the subtlety of the brushwork, how the artist moves from white to black and handles scales of grey—things that you or I might not think about. He might look at the quality of the canvas, how it is stretched, how the artist has used light. Likewise, when I look at a photo, I might see things you wouldn't. After a quarter century of taking photos, I might know what lens was used, what speed and shutter, film stock, printing process, filters...and a host of other things someone else cannot know, simply because they have not been taught much about these things.

Sometimes this thought process can get in the way of simply opening your heart and responding to the message, so I intentionally stay away from these kinds of responses. I like having the ability to use this knowledge if I feel a positive emotional response to a photo; however, unless I feel a strong emotional response, I don't much care how it was taken.

When I go into a house that I like, and I feel good there, I pay more attention to the kinds of wood used, the shape of things, the kind of plaster on the walls. I notice the floors, the light fixtures, the kitchen and bathrooms. I like having some basic knowledge with which to evaluate how things were done but, if I don't like the house or feel good in it, I have no use for this information.

When Sidi looks at another human being, he has vast resources and knowledge to evaluate their station. The same holds true when he looks at what is going on around him. He sees things in the moment that others do not see; he sees what is behind things because he can see the presence of Allah so deeply. When he looks at an illness in someone, he sees not just the problem, but the cause and solution as well. As I have mentioned, I am not in a station to know much about what Sidi sees, but I know he sees a lot— as the experience with my Dad points out.

As I think now about that breakfast with Maryam, it is as vivid as if it happened yesterday. I can feel all the seeds Sidi planted in me, which have nourished me over the years, still adding substance to what I digested that morning, and providing fruit from that tree to feed me. **Because of all that was behind and hidden inside that meal, the breakfast I ate that morning still provides nourishment to me today, unlike**

many other meals that have left me hungry only a few hours later.

The tie of the deep love that Sidi gives is stronger than that of blood. I have seen my blood father maybe three times in my life; my ties to him are nothing compared to the man who brought me up, and whom I think of as my Dad. And the ties to him, as strong as they are, are nothing compared to the ties I feel with Sidi. I once told a beloved that, if Sidi asked me to put out my arm because he wanted to chop off my hand, I would not ask why. I think that, if he asked me to give my life, I wouldn't ask why—because I would only be giving him back the life he gave me.

As we progress spiritually, we are asked to let go of our selves, our personality; we are asked to die to the material world, and to live in God alone. This annihilation is known as fana, and this fana comes in three stages. The first is in the shaykh; the second is in the holy prophet Muhammad, may peace and blessings be upon them both; the third is in Allah. This is the seventh station of the soul. From *Music of the Soul*, this is the message:

> *If you do not love all things, and know the meaning of the special love in the religion of God, you do not understand any of His truth. Before, you did not drink the wine of the special way of Allah. Now you are intoxicated by the wine, but this is the intoxication of love. This is the quality you lived in from the beginning, before the creation, before Allah created anything. Now you find Him in everything, in*

every face, everywhere; and there is nothing like Him. He is
in all the creation, and you can know this, in this station.
You can walk, you can fly, but with the light, with the holy
self, and with the love. You can find all the knowledge of
Allah if you can open the secret love, to know the complete
human being — Insan al-Kamil. He is the complete light of
Allah, and he is the eye of Allah. Continue and change
everything, and to clean your soul, and to know. This is the
deep station, and a long station. You need to leave
everything behind to reach the heart of the soul, and this
heart is the holy house of Allah.

Let's look at this a bit. **"If you do not love all things" means,**
to me, that you must see the face of Allah in and behind
every single thing you look at. This face was in the breakfast
I ate with Maryam; it was in my father, even though we
thought and felt so differently; it was in Nathalie, even
though I couldn't see beyond the outside picture. It's not just
in what I like; it's in what I don't like. It is everywhere and in
everything. Some people do as I have done for much of my
life—they allow their nafs to obscure this light. But when you
obscure this light, you also block and limit your own vision
and ability to see grace in others.

While your heart is covered with rust, it obscures your own
vision, especially the eye of your heart, which is the only
eye that can see things in the way of which Sidi speaks.
There is no way to see or experience the annihilation while
your heart is covered with rust. I learned that I didn't need
Nathalie to change in order to reach happiness; I needed to

change myself, and to die to the desires I felt around the
pictures I had of our life and how I thought it should be.
Then the station she was in would not affect my station, and I
could love her, regardless of whether she loved me back. **I
cannot imagine that any of us love Sidi as much as he loves
us, because our hearts are not as open as his.**

Not only must you see and surrender to the perfect man, the
insan al-kamil who is the guide; you must also surrender to
the original perfect man, our master, our messenger, the
carrier of the glorious Koran, the distributor of the light, the
prophet of the love, our beloved Muhammad, may peace and
blessings follow him and his followers always. You must find
and surrender to your own divine perfection, and you must
see and surrender to the divine perfection inherent in all the
creations of Allah. Until you see no difference between
anyone else's heart and your own, you are creating and living
in separation, and cannot touch the core of this station. I
believe this kind of station is realized one step at a time. Only
the most blessed are able to live in such a state; only the
prophets and messengers carried this kind of light. Sidi says:

> *Spirit and body must be united in one life. This is why
> our path is the path of unity: because we unite
> everything into one.*

To me, when Sidi writes of spirit and body being united, it
carries the same meaning as when he says to love everything,
because the unity of which he speaks is not possible without
the love. Uniting everything into one means that we unify all

our individual essences, and our hearts with all other hearts. Offering our selves (our nafs) as a sacrifice is a high form of prayer. Eventually, as we arrive in moments of fana, all of our selves disappear as Allah embraces us and takes us into His arms. This experience is the real garden; this is where the real life begins. Abraham was willing to offer God what was most precious to his own heart, and we must be willing to do the same if we wish to reach an elevated station. With this kind of surrender we become more illuminated with divine light, and thus achieve more freedom from self-centered attitudes.

All you need is one moment. People have strayed from the teachings of heaven, of divinity. They are stuck with the world of creation, amassing wealth, and drink and sleeping. They kill each other, destroy their homes, stop others from what they want because they want it for themselves. They have abandoned the teachings of God. We have been created male and female and as different peoples and tribes so that we may know each other. The best are those who are aware of Allah. Through your hand Allah, He moves. When you talk, He speaks. Your tongue does not speak but Allah He speaks through your tongue. When you give, the giver is Allah. You are not, but through you He gives. So you want to give completely and to not keep or stop with any pictures or illusions, but to go deeper. Then you will not see in front of you, you will not see behind you. For in that moment you are giving love to yourself, from yourself. This is a very holy station.

You are so weak. You have come from a drop of sperm. **Why did God create you? He created you to know yourself because you carry within you the divine secrets.** *You are a container, more than a container. You are a holy container. He made you to carry the message of the truth to all human beings. Everything that is in existence is sacred. Do not spend time or support those who defile this holy existence. Remove the cover of your heart to see what is inside your heart.*

As Sidi sat with me that day, and the truth flowed from his heart, I could feel myself ready to surrender more and more. Every cell of my body resonated with his energy and love, but I did feel fear about whether I could sustain this magic when he was not sitting next to me. I looked over at Maryam, and could feel her deep devotion. She hung on every word, was transfixed by him; I thought about how many years she had been able to sit with Sidi, and how fantastic it was to see her still like a child in many ways. How many nights did she get to share in this magical outpouring? Sidi spoke:

Always be in worship so every act is for Allah. Sincerity gives birth to love. Be in the adab with everyone who comes to you, for they are all manifestations of Allah. You have to go to your divine self to see the divine. You have to go to the fana, because you can't take divine love in your humanity. When you are sincere, when you follow this way, when you give everything to Allah, the pleasure of this path never comes to an end.

As I listened, I felt truly ready to give up everything. As I write these words, I wonder why I have held back as much as I have. These words may not be exactly what he said in that moment, but they are the essence of what he teaches, and I have heard them from him again and again over the years. I have spent so much time going over what he said and, still today, write out teachings multiple times. As I have said before, I ask myself so often how Sidi would do things, or what he would say, that I believe I have a feeling as to what those responses would be.

Of course, the moment I start to think Sidi is a certain way, I am immediately humbled when he responds in a different manner. But one thing never, ever changes: the love that is always present. In this love I taste Allah, and I am still as amazed by him today—how, after all these years, when I sit with him, just like Maryam did that night in the zawiyah, every moment is still so magical, so full of the divine, such a great taste of what proximity to Allah must feel like.

When Sidi comes to the U.S., I travel with him a lot, and read the teachings to beloveds. Sometimes I read the same teaching over and over as we move from one group to the next. And every time, I find something new, something I didn't catch before. Often, I will gain new clarity about some circumstance of my life. The idea of how I would write this story was brought about from these experiences.

I might be reading from *The Secret of the Love of God*, or one of the stations, and suddenly see how the teaching explains what is going on in some area of my life. One thing that strongly impacts me is how often Sidi will repeat a certain thing. (At least, this is what I hear.) Sometimes, at the end of one of his visits, I will hear beloveds sharing what they thought was the gist of the teaching for those months, and it is rare to ever hear the same answer. One summer, every time he said the word *patience*, I felt he was talking directly to me. Sidi always talks about patience but, for some reason it felt to me that he repeated it more often than other times. However, when he returned the next summer, I still heard the word patience used all the time. I think I felt that way because I was ready to accept more of the teaching about patience, and start to apply patience in my walking.

I certainly heard a lot about patience back in Jerusalem; in the letters I exchanged with Sidi for years through Maryam, he always counseled me to be patient. But at that time, I was unable. Every hour of waiting to see what Nathalie would do seemed like an eternity. I was impatient to write more teachings. I wanted all the answers, and I wanted them now.

I have always been fascinated with magic, and there is magic in everything if we learn to see it. I even got interested in card magic, and magic with objects, and spent a lot of time looking into this art form. This kind of magic is interesting in that the art lies in what remains unseen. In most kinds of art, the art is in what you see—the beauty and grace of a ballet dancer, the way a film is put together—but in card magic, the art is in what you don't see. And this is close to what I experience with the magic in Sidi. Where the real magic lies, where the art is found, is in the hidden and unseen depths of his essence. **The highest and most noble art is for me the art that we make of our lives. Sidi is a master at guiding us all to a higher expression of ourselves, and thus to a more creative and nobler fulfillment of our purpose.**

> *One must be patient. They must persevere in patience. The messenger of Allah, may the blessings and peace of Allah be upon him, said, "Faith is comprised of two things, one half is patience and the other half is gratitude." This hadith indicates that patience is one of the attributes of Allah and not a human quality. The prophet also said, "No one has patience and endures more than Allah." Be patient, do not try to eat the whole apple in one bite, and trust Allah, for He loves you more than you love yourself.*

And as always during that time, I tried to get in one more question about Nathalie and what would happen. He responded:

> *Surely you are different from her. Your spirit is a part of the spirit of your Beloved whom you love, and He loves you. For that He wants you to be strong, and to continue walking, and not to look to any side; and to remember His name in His perfect way. I am sure He will not leave you alone. In any way I am with you and I won't leave you for one moment. But walk, then you see through the remembering of the name of Allah the real help; and also through the teachings that you have. Allah blesses you and He blesses all your children.*

And as he took his leave, I returned to my room, wondering how I could feel so good and so bad at the same time.

Pictures and Illusions

*T*he next day I re-launched my efforts to get some photocopies of the teachings to take back with me, so that I wouldn't leave behind things I knew I needed. I made absolutely no headway with Maryam, as she simply kept repeating, "Oh no, my beloved. Sidi never allows the teachings to be copied by machine. This has to be done by hand." So I made a mental note to bring it up with Sidi, to tell him why I wanted and needed to make some photocopies of the teachings.

This was the day I made my first visit to the holy site of the al-Aqsa mosque, and spent some time with Sidi in his office. Almost the first thing I brought up was that I was working day and night to copy the teachings, and was feeling desperate because I knew I had to return to my children before I could finish writing everything. And I wanted to have all the teachings so that I could continue my walking. I also wanted to read them to my children, and share them with other friends that I knew would want to know about the message.

I talked to him about all the lost souls in the U.S. who had sought answers for years and, like me, had bounced from teacher to guru, in and out of all the different paths. I said they were all seeking true guidance from a real guide, but had no idea where to turn. I said he should come to the U.S., and that I could introduce him to people like me who might help spread his message of the love and the mercy, the peace and the justice.

But he said there was no permission yet for him to leave Jerusalem, and that he could not move without the order from Allah. So I asked him again about copying the teachings, and he said:

> Be patient; write as much as you can. This is our way and this is all that Allah gives permission for.

I wasn't happy with the response, but I also realized he hadn't definitively said no—and even if he had, I planned to continue asking. After all, the teachings talked about patience and perseverance, and I considered myself a pretty fast learner in some things.

Visiting Sidi in the mosque and praying there was a special experience, but I am ashamed to say I didn't value it at the time. I was obsessed with my situation, and with figuring out a way to take more of the teachings back with me. This singular focus has served me amazingly well in some instances; at the same time, however, it has kept me from experiences from which I might have benefited, had I given them more consideration.

Also, my knowledge and understanding of Islam was so small, I didn't realize al-Aqsa was the third most important site for Muslims, behind only Mecca and Medina. This was some of the most cherished and special real estate in the world—and Sidi had his own private little building that held his office, where people steadily dropped in to ask his counsel or to receive his baraka (grace). He was a simple and humble man, and he received all visitors with the same open heart, whether they were poor or rich, male or female. It was quite extraordinary to witness Sidi speaking in front of hundreds of thousands of people, as well as the television cameras that were there. It was a Friday, and he was giving the khutbah, which is the sermon or oration given at the noon prayer. The Koran asks all Muslims to leave their affairs and hasten to the remembrance of Allah at this time, so the entire mosque was full, and tens of thousands more were gathered in the courtyard. This was my first experience with a khutbah. As Sidi spoke in Arabic, I didn't understand a word. But he spoke passionately, and with power.

Even though I wasn't fully present during these moments, they were to have a profound and lasting effect on me. I would later resonate not only with what happened at al-Aqsa, but with my entire experience in Jerusalem, in a way that transformed me and my life. I was just too focused on myself, and it is true that nothing will keep you more separated from the love and the unity than focusing all your attention on yourself. Looking back it seems obvious, and even kind of simple—but for me, it took years and years of painful struggle. Even today, even though I know I shouldn't do it, I do not always follow my own advice, much less Sidi's.

I had no doubt that trip to Jerusalem to spend time with Sidi would change my life. I've wondered much about this.

People often change their outside forms as they move through life, maybe going from one style of dress to another. I certainly have. Sometimes, you can't recognize the person for who they were before. I know I have changed a lot—not only the outside picture, but how I think and feel and react. And I wonder: Am I the same person? When my kids look at photos of me when I was much younger, they have a good laugh. If I properly understand what Sidi has taught me, I believe he saw things in me that no one else had, and he watered the seeds that allowed me to grow closer to who I was created to be. When he looked at me and said he saw "beauty," he brought something to life that needed the water of love, both his and my own. He has allowed me the grace of feeling my own "specialness." So even though the outside picture changed, perhaps the original person just came out of hiding.

I grew up thinking that, as you grew older, you automatically became wiser—that you would be able to figure out more about the purpose of life and how it worked. Parents would say you had to do what they wanted you to do, to obey them, because they were older and knew better. In my case, the older I get, the more I realize I haven't figured out as much as I expected. But I have fallen more in love with the mystery and magic of all that is unseen.

When Sidi looks at things he sees so much more…but he also has the inside truth and the complete teachings to deal with everything he sees. I walked through a refugee camp once in Bangladesh back in the 1970s, and was overcome by the suffering I saw. I have felt the same thing walking in

Jerusalem, watching the absolutely horrible way people are treated there. As I have traveled extensively, I have seen a lot of suffering. But I am not constantly aware of it, as Sidi is; he lives with others' suffering and pain daily. People come to him, just as I did, with broken hearts and broken bodies—without Allah's wisdom, I think there would be no way for him to contain all the people he does, and all their suffering and pain. And even when he is alone, his spirit travels to dark places, into which he sends love and light.

This is why it is so important to do the practices, study the teachings, practice repeating the name, continue to open the heart so more love flows, and become a bigger person: Then you can be part of the solution, not part of the problem. This is just one of the reasons Sidi gives so much to so many people. He has also said that all the human limbs are tools for an unfinished business, so we must take care of all aspects of ourselves, both internal and external.

In this way he can leverage himself, so that more people can be helped. Sidi works with a large group of people in the U.S. who have done truly amazing work in promoting his teachings and introducing others to this path. Each beloved plays a special part in the overall picture of things, bringing unique talents and abilities; when they are all together, they create a truly amazing team. Sidi oversees everything, and contains every heart with a skill I have never encountered elsewhere.

I sometimes feel awkward in writing this story because I want it to be honest, and I know that both Sidi and Allah will know of every inconsistency, any part of me that tries to "bluff," and any falsehoods. This has caused me to stop more than once. In fact, there was a period of months, during which I was unable to move forward at all because of this fear. Sometimes, as Sidi and I talked on the phone, he would mention that he'd finished writing a new book, and I could see he was the true son of his moment. When he told me recently that he had just finished a second book, I felt so ashamed of myself that I decided to move forward, no matter what. I have made real progress as I move toward completion of this book. The patience and perseverance he said I would need to get through my situation with Nathalie have been useful in every other area of my life as well. Sidi's teachings are useful if you pay close attention, and use the written or spoken words in your daily actions.

Many years ago, I went with Jason and Jessica, my two oldest kids, to a karate class while we were living in Texas. (This was about 20 years ago.) We always started the class by working out, and some of the exercises, such as the pushups, were quite painful for me. The instructor explained the importance of these exercises was that they stretched your body's abilities—but you had to go through some painful moments to get to the place where your body could do more. "What you are looking for is on the other side of the pain," he said. And so I have had to go through discomfort, doubt and fear to find what I am looking for, which is to share these teachings with you. In a sense, doing these conditioning exercises was just another example of how we have to build the container of our selves, for any path we choose to follow.

Look at what athletes go through; yet their physical strength is nothing compared to the spiritual strength of Sidi.

Because the purpose of this book is to share with you how I use the teachings in my daily life—at least I think that's the purpose, but Sidi may see something different—I want to spend a bit more time with this moment in the mosque, and how being there with Sidi has impacted me. I have a tremendous attraction to the Arab culture, which developed many years before I met Sidi in the body. At every opportunity, I traveled into this culture, never knowing that one day I would become so committed to Islam and so passionate about Sidi and the prophet, may peace and blessings be upon them, and the holy Koran.

The specialness of that day, of sitting in the mosque and visiting other places on that holy site as Sidi explained their history, grew over the following years. I might be walking someone through my house, giving a tour, and feel almost foolish—showing off the dunya things, of which I was proud—as I remembered the teachings Sidi shared as we walked around the mosque, and the pride he felt in what Allah had built.

It wasn't just the places, the architecture, the beauty in the shape of everything, the lights, the furniture, and objects that I was drawn to. It was the people, and the character they all displayed in their faces. I wanted to know everyone. In fact, I want to share an amusing story.

Years later, when I was divorced from Nathalie and living on my own, Sidi and I were in Washington at an Islam conference. On a Friday we went into a huge room to pray the noontime prayer. There was a crowd of people but, in one area, I saw a dozen or so completely veiled women wearing beautiful blue robes. They came from Africa, and I was attracted to their black skin framed by the blue fabric.

When I had lived in France, I heard people say that the best way to learn French was "on the pillow"—if you had a lover who didn't speak English, you would learn French pretty quickly. So I thought that, if I found a veiled woman of the Koran (a real Muslim), I could learn more of this culture and marry her. Then I would be able to walk faster.

After the prayer, while walking with Sidi, I mentioned that I had thought these women beautiful. I asked what he thought about me finding a bride who resembled one of these women. I thought he might be pleased with this idea. So I mentioned it and then asked, "Is that a picture, Sidi?" He answered:

A very big picture, Salih.

I laugh about it now, but it was a big awakening for me in many ways. To this day, I stop too much with the outside images of people, instead of looking at the deep, inside heart. But if you are like me and want to break as many pictures as possible, Sidi is the master at helping one get over illusions.

I have been in many mosques since that day, have even returned to al-Aqsa a number of times, but there is still the imprint of that first visit. Before, I had never prayed with perhaps a quarter of a million people. It expanded my horizons exponentially. Even today, when I pray alone, I feel thousands of others praying with me, because everyone in the same time zone prays so close to a certain time. When I fast during Ramadan, I have the feeling of a shared experience with literally millions of people worldwide, and it creates a feeling of closeness and family that I've never felt anywhere else. When I hear a call to prayer, I feel that call touching a lot more hearts than just mine. And in that time of prayer, with everyone side by side, I do feel the truth of *one heart, one body, one mind and one soul.*

I returned to the zawiyah with Maryam with an even stronger desire to learn more about Islam and how to pray properly. But I was still almost obsessed with copying as many teachings as I could because, though I hadn't given up on getting copies of the teachings, I was not at all sure I would succeed. So I wrote for nearly the rest of the day, until Sidi returned. I was still overly tired, and depressed about my situation, and it seemed like such a long time since I had left the U.S. and had any contact with Nathalie. I had been in touch with the kids and all was well there; a good friend who also had children was staying at the house, so everyone was having a good time.

As I studied and wrote the teachings, I didn't feel that I was establishing new patterns, so much as illuminating some of

the old ones. I sensed the world was more infinite than I had
dreamed, and much was hidden from me in my own universe that I had yet to discover. I was tuning in to things that
were quite formless, so I could not think about them and put
them into words—but feelings were moving within me, and
long-dormant parts of my being were coming awake. I was,
in a sense, giving birth to a new creation. The seeds of this
creation were miraculously kept alive by the divine mercy
and compassion of Allah. Sidi was watering them with the
magic of his love, giving them more life. He could obviously
see more in me than I saw in myself. This is true even today.

Allah is a continuous lover who never stops feeding our
hearts. The mind is for gathering information, so I had to
trust my heart for true revelation. In my state, it would not be
wise to allow the mind to dictate decisions. Sidi had said that,
when we step on the path, the time is no longer ours, but
Allah's, so we should be sure not to waste it. When he came
to see me in the evening, I was obviously still preoccupied by
my situation with Nathalie.

> *Be patient. Until when you see the real thing that happens
> for this love. This is the first step. You will come to know
> more and more and more and more; then you will see the
> real love come thru close beloveds who love you. Anyone
> who loves you opens his heart for you because he loves you.
> This is the real thing. See the door open for this love, and
> try to open your heart for this door. I guide you to the
> straight path. I open the door of love for you. This is what
> God wants me to give to all my beloved children.*

It is important to cross through the door and drink, not wait until you have lost everything. All the different stations are from the nafs, not from Allah, and there are many different stations. When you walk, Allah changes nafs to be pure and only for His love. Very important to destroy the pictures. Allah, He opens all the doors through your brothers and sisters. Go through this door and drink from the source of this love. Be strong and be soft and not wait until everything be finished. Take your chance, not worry about anything. Give yourself life.

Not wait, you or her. I give you the deep yearning, and I give her also.

This is the word of Allah. I am a very poor slave of Allah. Without permission from Allah I not talk. This is from the heart of Allah direct to her, to help her.

Leave her until she stop everything and she come to you and she say, "Yes, I am ready for your love." If she says yes this means she is completely right. If she not say that, it means she like to kill the love between you. Very important to understand that.

"Maybe she sees I need to change, Sidi. Because I have pictures."

I know you, Salih. You are better than pure. Allah, He shows me. I not say for you. This is what Allah, He shows me. What you are.

"I doubt it," I said. "I don't feel pure. I feel I have all these pictures, and I want what I think is best for me, and I feel as if I know what's best for her. And this doesn't feel right, but I can't help it."

You are special beloved for Allah. You are very pure. Not lose this pure, not throw this pure away for who not understand and who not want to take it. This is what Allah He shows me. Not think, not think, not think. Stop thinking. Not listen for any voice. This is important.

This particular conversation was truly powerful and healing to my heart. Sidi's words, though I had a hard time accepting them—and I'm not sure I totally believed them—were another example of the seeds he was watering. Sidi later taught me that there are qualities Allah places in all of humanity, which in many cases lie dormant, and it was these qualities he was nurturing in me. He saw what I couldn't see; my discovery of these qualities came through as feelings in my heart before they manifested as thoughts in my mind.

It says in *Al-Wazifatu l-Mashishiyyah*, which Sidi gave me to read, study, and recite: "The understanding of the secret (which had been put in him, Muhammad, peace and blessings be upon him) was made impossible for every other created being whose understanding is very small. Yet each one's inability to understand suffices him." We can only drink from the ocean of the secrets according to our capacity to understand. I learned that, if I was to realize even a portion of the limitless bounties with which Allah graces our existence, I had a lot of work to do. In Allah's infinite love, He allows us to live with our limited understanding until we are ready to wake, and take the path. We can function in the material world with this limited understanding, but we don't get the full, sweet taste of the world of the spirit.

I stayed up late again, writing as much as I could. When my hand cramped, I would stop and stumble through some attempts at praying properly. But because I was so concerned with how I was doing things, I feel I didn't get much benefit. Sidi was always encouraging around this; he told me Allah looked at the intent and sincerity in my heart, rather than if my actions and pronunciation were perfect. This brought relief, but also concerned me, because he made clear that nothing was hidden from Allah, and I was pretty ashamed of my lack of sincerity many times during prayers. I found my mind wandering; I knew that I might appear devout on the outside, and my tongue may recite the prayer, but my mind was thinking of something else. I still wrestle with this today.

One thing he mentioned, which I thought a lot about, was the love from the real beloveds. Nura and Tarik, the ones who sent me to Sidi, were the people I most trusted and most loved, and they were deep and real beloveds. It was their love and support that carried me through the most troubled times. And because they knew Sidi and the teachings, they remained a strong connection for me. When I returned, I met another beloved in Santa Fe, Mu'Mina, who also was deeply and lovingly supportive, and brought much love and light into my life. Sadly, I remained caught up in my pictures and, in this confusion, was not able to follow Sidi's instructions. I sipped at the cup they offered, when I should have gulped down every drop. The message was so clear; I just couldn't open my heart.

In *The Station of the Love*, Sidi remarks:

> *Allah said, "Say, if you love Allah, follow me, then Allah will love you." The messenger, may the peace and blessings of Allah be upon him, related in Hadith Qudsi, "My slave approaches me with additional prayers until I love him, and when I love him, I become his hearing, his seeing, his tongue and his hand; in Me he hears, through Me he sees, by Me he speaks, and by Me he strikes."*

> *Know that there are two kinds of love: The love of the slave for the Allah, and the love of Allah for the slave. The love of the slave for Allah is in his faith. The love of Allah for the slave is placed in the following of the beloved. Allah says, "Say: 'If you love Allah, follow me and Allah will love you.'"* **A believer has a stronger love for Allah than for anything else, and love increases with the increase of faith.** *The lover follows the prophet, may the peace and blessings of Allah be upon him, according to the measure of his love, and Allah loves the believer according to the measure of his following the beloved prophet.*

One of the things Sidi means here is that there is no similarity between the human and divine, in that we are totally dependent on God, while He is totally independent of us. We should not mistake the creator for the creation. This theme recurs throughout Sidi's teachings.

What all this meant to me is that, as long as I followed my pictures, I remained at a distance from the real love. I did not have enough faith or a strong enough love for Allah to let go of the attachments to the material world; my mind still told me they were my security blanket. Yet the real love has definitely increased as my faith has, and I know no words to describe the love I now feel. Every word Sidi writes is true. I could have read these words a hundred, even a thousand times, but my heart was not ready to accept them. So they remained something I could repeat, but could not manifest.

This was true of much of what he told me then, and in the years to come. It was all there in the teachings; it was in the words he spoke; it was in conversations we would have over the phone. Yet no matter how many times he told me the same thing, it took a long time to accept the message and start living the teachings. I can only imagine how frustrating this must have been for the beloveds who tried so valiantly to help, and opened their hearts so wide.

When Sidi speaks truth, it would be as if he threw seeds upon a rock, were there no beloveds in whom to plant the seeds. He says over and over how important the beloveds are to him, yet I could not see it. All I could see was my self—and this intense focus on my self created a lot of pain that lasted a long time. These teachings, along with everything that comes with them, are a life raft in an ocean of tidal waves; they are the water in an immense and lonely desert. A few sentences, completely understood and digested—and then applied in our lives—can change everything.

Letting Go and Trusting

My visit was coming to an end. I had to return to my children and, though the visit had been short, I felt I had a lot to absorb and work with. If not for the children, I could easily have stayed for months. I had no desire to work, especially since it usually meant being on location, and that meant leaving the kids again. But I knew in my heart, especially with all Sidi had said about the importance of being earth to the children, that I would have to re-evaluate how I made a living. I could sense that my whole life was going to change. Things simply were not ever going to be the same again.

This was difficult in many ways, because I had thought I was pretty happy, and it was hard to let go of all the pictures. Looking back as I write this, I can only stare in disbelief at those times. I live such a quiet life now, hardly ever going out. I have changed professions, my kids are grown, and I have grown, for which I thank Allah. I would not find enjoyment in what I did before; in fact, I think it would feel uncomfortable and drive me nuts. I am thankful for all the doors that opened, and I prefer my life now to the one I led before. All the while, I am grateful for every step that brought me to Sidi's presence and teachings.

There was still one thing I wanted to do before I left: make copies of the teachings I had not yet written, so that I could continue to write them when I got home. Also, I hadn't even read over half the teachings, and this occupied my mind. I felt this was something I wanted badly, and that the teachings would be wonderful to have, not only for me but for many others. Maryam was absolutely against this, in respect for Sidi's wishes. But I still felt there was a chance with him because, although he had not said yes, he had not said no either. I spent quite a lot of time trying to come up with good reasons why I thought Sidi should allow me to copy the teachings. Yet I knew that, if Allah did not give him permission, there was no way it would happen. I thought about the teachings, and how they mentioned the importance of himma, or yearning...I had a lot of yearning to get some photocopies. So I started thinking of how I could ask in a way that would increase my chances of getting a yes.

I don't think the outcome was in my hands at all, but I do feel my passion for wanting to have the teachings with me in Santa Fe opened my heart in some way; and the degree to which I could open my heart would play a big part in Sidi maybe saying yes. All the things he had said to me about trust and patience were going in one ear and out the other, because I wanted things resolved quickly. I wanted Nathalie to come back; I wanted her to love me and leave the other men. And I wanted this now, not tomorrow. Every hour I waited seemed like an eternity, and I didn't have the faith or the trust to let patience have a place in my life.

I think I mentioned before that I've always felt one of my strongest assets is being the "son of my moment," getting things done quickly and efficiently. This impatience and the inability to wait for things were detrimental in many ways, but I figured that, if I pushed hard enough for what I wanted, I could get it. I had always felt pretty successful in life, and able to have what I wanted. But now I was in uncharted waters, with a wife who was going to decide for herself, and a guide who was not going to respond to my control issues.

I learned from Sidi that "the journey is the journey," and that one must sometimes accept the pace at which things happen. You don't quit halfway to your destination just because it is taking time, especially when you know ahead of time that it will take a certain number of hours to get there. You expect the trip to take time. I was going to have to accept the time it would take to get to a new place, and it would do no good to quit on the way.

On the day I left, I planned to take a taxi back to the airport in Tel Aviv, and was scheduled to leave in the late morning. When I woke that day, I still didn't have permission from Sidi to copy the teachings. I had hardly slept the whole night; instead, I frantically wrote as much as I could. When my hand cramped, I would speed-read as many of the teachings as possible. I wanted every drop; I wanted the knowing; I wanted freedom from the pain. And I wanted it now.

I knew Sidi would come to say goodbye before he left for the mosque. The previous night, I had been afraid to ask again about the teachings...I think I was scared he would say no. His message that night was still the same:

*Be in the beauty, be the goodness, love goodness and offer
peace, love and mercy for all creation. Follow all His orders.
Worship the creator and not creation. Follow this path. All
the prophets are children of the Sufi way. The Sufi way is
described in three words: letting go and beautifying.*

I asked him what he meant by that. "Do you mean to let go
of Nathalie?" And he said:

*Letting go means to let go of every thing unpleasing to
Allah. Let go of the dunya and all its evils. Allah made all
evil in one house, and the key to it is love of this world, and
he made all the good acts in one house, and the key to it is
abstinence. Allah does not say no to the good things of this
world, so let go of what He doesn't like, such as hurting
people, and corruption.*

*The spirit and the body need to be united in one life. It is
the heart and soul that make the body move. Without Allah
you could not lift your finger. Our path is the path of unity
and we unite everything into one. The people of our path
make no discrimination between the prophets. Moses, Jesus,
Abraham are all brothers and they all carry the same
message from Allah, the message of unity.*

*Use the name. The name can be a fire that burns away
imperfections and helps to lift the dark veils. Bringing
happiness to others is one of the best things. Treat their
hearts as you want your heart to be treated. True giving is
surrendering to others what is most precious to you.*

*Allah wants you always to be with Him, face to face, and to
carry His message and to give the love, the peace and the
mercy for each other, for everyone, if you know them or
don't know them. Give love to the animals, and the trees,
and not just the human beings. Be honest, be truthful, be
sincere in every transaction and always walk straight. You
show your honesty to Allah by being honest with others. Be
straight with Allah by being straight with others.*

I could have listened for hours. There is a certain peace I feel
in my heart when Sidi talks. Even just sitting with him opens
my heart, and allows me glimpses of greater possibilities.

*Many names are gathered in one name. And all the
different people, all the differences in human beings are
there for us to know our selves. Be busy with your own
remembrance. **Use the love to traverse all the stations.
How can you traverse the stations of the heart
without opening your heart and giving the love? Give
with a divine heart so that you may receive with a
divine heart. There is one soul, not divisible, and it
can only give to itself.** Don't stop with the humanity. Go
on to the everlasting life. Realize who faces you. If you have
faith in Allah today, then today you can enter into the
garden. Give everything now, to take everything now.*

There it was again. He was clearly telling me to be the "son
of my moment," and not wait until tomorrow. We must have
faith behind every action, and give thanks and constant
remembrance to Allah. Sidi is always rigorous about the

fundamentals of the practices, and relentless in repeating the things we must do to earn the benefits of this path. In order to have anything of value we must first surrender. This is the core of Islam, the very meaning of the word. In surrendering, we are able to disappear. For me, Islam is about giving up who I am and surrendering my limited self, in return for the awesome possibilities that exist in the richer life of the spirit.

The prophet himself, peace and blessings be upon him, was incredibly pure in life. When I search for inspiration for my own behavior, I know where to look. Both he and Sidi, may Allah bless and sanctify their secret, are examples of the awesome possibilities of our potential. There are countless other examples throughout Sidi's books, and the rest of mystical and spiritual literature. We can learn and grow by patterning ourselves after these elevated individuals.

Plant the seed of the deep and the real love in your heart, Salih, and nurture this seed with the living water of the remembrance. Then this seed will grow into a tree of love and this tree will give you fruits of its own. This tree of love gives its fruit to everyone without asking why or what, without looking at their color or their religion, because every human is the brother and sister of every other human being whether they like it or not. That is a fact of life.

This is the Sufi way. This is the message that every prophet carried and this message gives to every human being knowledge of their own reality. We must all say no to wars, no to killing, no to destruction and burning of homes, and no to the destruction of humanity. And we must say yes to the peace, and the love and the mercy and the justice. We must take away the resources destructive to humanity and put those resources into things that are beneficial to humanity. We must put our resources into things that are useful, to help those in need of the basic things they need to live. And we can do this by planting the seed of love in every heart that we can encounter.

It is time for you to return home and carry this message. Do not throw your love upon things that do not feed your heart. Leave Nathalie until she is ready and give your love to your holy children. Be with beloveds of the family of Allah. Sit with them at the table of the real food. Drink from them, and open your heart so that they can drink from you. This is the real love, and I thank Allah for this, when He shows me how beautiful is this family. Allah loves you more than you love yourself. And I will be always with you. I will not leave you for one second.

I will travel with you in all your stations and your states. I feel deeply all that you feel. Stay away from the pictures which come at you from every direction, both from the outside which are easy to recognize, and from the inside which are much deeper and more subtle, and more difficult sometimes to leave, because they lie there, hidden and covered over with many layers which cover them from our eyes. The eye of Allah sees everything, and He shows me, and I will help you build the house of Allah in your heart.

There are many people crying and suffering in the darkness. Allah puts His beloveds to be the lamp for everyone who has the eyes to see, and to help them see a way out of the darkness of the dunya. Give the message for the beloveds in America. Many, many people are thirsty to know the truth of the real Islam. The religion of unity of all the prophets. I ask Allah to keep me to be His slave and give me strength to give.

We are all from one father and there is no difference between black and white, slave or king. All of those are from clay and they return to clay. It is important for everyone to love one another and help one another, and not fight, and be one people under the flag of the real Islam. This message carries the reality of the essence of Allah; it carries the complete message, what everyone, all people, they need. The prophet, peace and blessings upon him, never said or taught to kill women and children. If anyone kills one person it's like he killed all the people. If someone gives life for one person it is like he gives life for all people. This is Islam. This way is not for killing but giving life. All the real sons of Abraham, Jew, Muslim or Christian, follow this tradition. I carry the message of the peace and the love and the mercy and the justice. This is the message direct from Allah, through my heart, and I give it to everyone who seeks to know the truth about their existence.

The human form is special because it can contain the divine tajalli (revelation). So carry and take care of this trust, and carry it by free will. We have all the divine words, all the revealed books, orders, and laws. By going against these orders you lose and suffer. Sing the divine song of la illaha illah la. All killing is a rebellion against the original contract of Allah. Adam gave birth to his mirror, exactly himself. So we come from one another. She is earth for him, and he is heaven for her. Heaven sends water, then earth gives birth to all couples. Both come representing the one light and both can carry the manifestation of divine revelation. You are both the house of Allah and it is not permissible for anyone to throw stones and break the glass of this house. This love is very holy and this holiness is your relationship with Allah.

We are Allah's charges, His representatives, and this life is given to us as a test to see which of us is best in our actions. Live for the good pleasure of Allah, inwardly detached from the material things. Live from the quality of gentleness. The best of acts is to lose sight of one's acts and to behold divine grace. Do not be in contradiction to the world of harmonious light and the pure disposition and essence of the soul. Behold the divine majesty in the station of the heart. **Walk within Allah's limits, and He will make it easy for you.**

Care about yourself, my beloved son. Leave everything else but Him and His way, follow every minute the messenger and helper He sends. Follow this way to be in the garden of the love and the peace and the mercy. I ask Allah that He shows you the straight path, without which there is no real life for us. Happiness has its source in divine love, which is

*within us. Success is hard if you don't look at it correctly.
See it as service and it becomes easy.* **Wake up wondering
what you can do to help heal others and this will
increase everything for you and you will find yourself
in the real garden.**

And with that Sidi took me in his arms, and I knew my time
with him on this trip was nearly complete. In that moment, I
felt the comfort and peace and hope that I had come to
Jerusalem hoping to find. I felt I was now connected, firmly
and strongly, to a source that could help me. I had found the
guide.

This feeling of peace lasted all of about ten minutes. By the
time I had returned to my room to pack, and started facing
the reality of returning to my life in Santa Fe, I had already
started making picture after picture of Nathalie's return.
When she next saw me, she would see a transformed and
enlightened man, instead of a whimpering and controlling
one. The teachings would make me so strong that I would be
irresistible. She would be overwhelmed with love for who I
was now. But, because this was in no way true, fear appeared
as my mind wandered down this path. Within minutes, I was
once again lost in sadness. I got up to pray. I thought that, if I
prayed and repeated the name, I would recapture the eupho-
ria I had in the presence of Sidi. But that was not to happen.

I thought then, and for many years after, that praying and
repeating the name didn't work for me. I would do the
practices but still feel depressed. The situation didn't seem to

be going the way I wanted, and I wasn't getting the outcome I thought I wanted. I have since learned that the name and the prayers are not insufficient—but what I brought to the table was. The insufficiencies were all within me. I would have to be more, grow more, and add more to the prayer. But in my room in Jerusalem I couldn't see that far. So I lay back on the bed, grabbed a handful of papers, and started reading again—all the while thinking of how I could convince Sidi to allow me to copy the teachings. I was running out of time. I would have only a few hours in the morning before leaving for the airport.

One of the things I've learned from being around Sidi is that fear usually starts with doubt; doubtful thoughts bring on fear. This fear then makes me feel stressed and anxious, and robs me of my energy and ability to repeat the name in a way that would bring me feelings of peace.

Let me use the experience I have just described as an example: I wanted to bring back some of the teachings, but doubted that Sidi would allow it. These doubts created fear, because they made me feel like I could fail. The fear created stress, which made me anxious, and thus unable to feel peaceful. So no matter how many times I repeated the name, I still came back to this unresolved issue.

One way I have always overcome fear in my life is to do the thing I fear. Because I work for myself from home, and have no one telling me what to do, I can get creative at postponing the things I need to do every day to be successful—such as making a certain number of calls. In the beginning I feared rejection, so I didn't want to make the calls. But instead of letting the fear hold me in its power, I plunged forward and made the calls. I simply made enough calls that the fear lost its hold on me. Likewise, I knew the only way I would get the teachings was to go through my doubts and fears, and keep asking.

This brings me to the most important thing about overcoming fear and doubt: *faith*. Fear and faith are polar opposites; they are two different views about the future, and how something will turn out. I am always inspired and moved by the depth of Sidi's faith. His faith in me has allowed my own faith to grow. I don't think faith and fear can truly exist at the same time in the same space because, if your faith is strong enough, fear cannot be present. I know Allah takes care of me. And the more I know this, the more I accept it, the more I feel it authentically and profoundly, the less fear and doubt I have. So when I trust and feel my faith, and use the name, I can touch places of peace that I cannot approach when I am in doubt and fear. **The presence of fear means there is an absence of love, or that one's love is blocked. While love is flowing, there is no place for fear.**

My faith is one of the main things lacking when I feel less in touch with the prayers and repeating the name. The prayer and the name don't change; they are constant. But my insides change...It's like eating an apple. Some days, depending on your level of hunger and awareness, the apple will taste better than on other days. Yes, some apples just taste better than others—but let's say you have a loaf of bread, in which all slices taste the same. On some days, that bread will still taste different.

When things around me don't feel good now, I tend to look inside myself, to see where I'm out of tune. In doing this, I can see where I'm reacting negatively, and how I can change this reaction. Thus, I can find the feelings I enjoy, without feeling I must change things outside of me—which I most likely could not change anyway.

I continued to read the teachings, still wondering if there would be a last-minute reprieve from Sidi. I felt some sadness about leaving; yet I was anxious to return home and see if Nathalie might respond more positively to me. As I write this, I realize how foolish all this was, thinking she would see changes in me and want to be with me again. First of all, I had a lot of work to do before these changes became a part of me; second, she was on a path that, in many ways, had little to do with me.

It takes time to see results when seeds are planted. If you walked in a garden that had just been planted, it would take a trained eye to see any change from the day before. You might notice the earth had been tilled, but I don't think there would be any way to see whether peas or corn were planted. It takes time before anything sprouts.

In my case, Sidi had tilled the earth and planted many things, as well as watered many dormant seeds, but it would be some time before any results could be seen. It is true, when he says, "Allah can change everything in an instant." Many things had been changed and set in motion during my visit, yet it would be years before I could witness the results. I don't know if Nathalie has ever known or experienced any of these changes. When we know people well, we can sometimes get stuck in the old pictures of how we knew them to be, and never accept the fact that they may have changed. This is often the case with parents and their children. If we feel one of our children usually acts in a certain way, it's sometimes challenging to see them in a different light. Both the parent and the child are caught in the pattern of the old picture. Change is not always easy to recognize, in ourselves or others.

Sidi has an ability to not only see the changes, but to see them before they are set into motion. He sees the potential that lies dormant or hidden, and knows how to guide us toward realizing it. This ability to see deeply is one of the things that has always amazed me about him; it applies to things in all the different worlds, even the material world. Once, when he was visiting my house in Santa Fe, the house next door to mine was for sale. Because one of the beloveds was looking for a property to buy, we walked with Sidi through the house. At one point, he stood in the living room, and mentioned this would not be a good house to buy because he could hear little animals in the walls. Later, when someone else bought the house and was remodeling it, they found extensive termite damage to all the wood. When I asked Sidi how he had seen or heard this, he said that he can

see a star in the sky even in the noonday sun. This kind of
inner vision is a gift from Allah for a chosen few, but I
mention it because it points the way to the potential of the
human being. Sidi carries an amazing amount of accumulated knowledge and adds to this a rich inner life. He sources
from a much broader and deeper place because he knows
how to access divine love. Last year, in one of his talks, Sidi
mentioned that human beings use only a small part of their
potential, but that we must be careful—though only using a
small part, we are still incredibly destructive as a whole to
our world. We abuse our planet and our resources at a
frightening speed.

I had a lot to digest from all Sidi had given me so far. A part
of me was looking forward to returning to my everyday
world, where I could put myself, now armed with some great
tools, to the test. I didn't know the worst had not yet come,
but I was blessed because I had someone who could contain
and hold me through the next stages. In a sense, my
ignorance was a blessing; if I had known what lay ahead, I
might not have had the strength to face it. As I mentioned
before, part of the wisdom and compassion of Sidi as a guide
is that he knows what should and shouldn't be revealed. I
have learned that these darkest moments were when my
greatest growth occurred.

Sidi has taught his beloveds not only about the power of
Allah, which governs all the universe; he has taught how to
discover that power within you. This is another reason Sidi
tells all of us "to keep the company of holy people; keep the

company of those who are seeking what you seek; keep the company of those who have made their migration to Allah." When one is in the presence of others who love and trust Allah, it is easier to tap into a positive and divine energy, because you can sense it in them. Just as Sidi manifests many qualities that beloveds are inspired to develop within themselves, we can also be inspired by any greatness we sense in others. Sidi has written in *The Path to Allah Most High*:

> *The creation cannot be outside His knowledge. People are not capable of earning anything except with His help. They are needy of Allah in all their actions. They need to be given a state and power from Him. Everything they have, including faith and acts of obedience, is because of His guidance and His giving them success, and His gentleness with His creation. Every wrong action they leave is because of His divine protection.*

So all praise is due to Allah, and it should be constant, and precede all else. I have learned that, before I can have more, I must give thanks for what I have. And that night, as I lay there thinking about my time in Jerusalem, and the precious moments I had spent with Sidi, my heart started overflowing with love and gratitude for all he had given me. I found myself forgetting about what I didn't have, and spent more time feeling blessed for what I had. It would be years before I would have this feeling again. I think one of the things that stunted my growth for so long is that I lost track of how important it is to not only feel grateful, but to express it.

If there had been a way for me to be grateful for all I had in my life, rather than crying about what I didn't have, I think I would have gotten through the painful years with more grace and elegance than I did. Of course, now that I'm removed from the pain, it's a lot easier to talk about these things and see solutions. But back there, in those moments, I just didn't allow myself to accept these truths.

When morning came, Sidi came downstairs on his way to the mosque, to say one last goodbye. I had been up for quite a while. Before he took leave, I thanked him for all he had given me. I had already completed my farewell in many ways. I had made a contribution to the poor, as he would not accept anything personally. From the beginning, Sidi taught that the way to open the heart to receiving is through giving. This is another way of showing praise and gratitude to Allah, and to prepare ourselves for any more gifts He may wish to grant us. I had received his teachings and his blessings, so I had only one thing more I wanted.

"Sidi," I said, "I feel bad that I didn't get to copy more of the teachings so I could study them and share them with some people in Santa Fe. Can I please make copies and bring them home with me? I promise to take good care of them and be very, very careful whom I show them to. This way I can continue my walking." And with a kind of amused twinkle in his eye, he said, "Okay, I trust you my son, and I know you can make good use of these teachings." And with that, he hugged me and took his leave.

I made sure Maryam had heard it was alright, and asked her where we could go to make the copies. She said she knew just the place, but we would have to move quickly if I wanted to make the copies and catch my plane. I was still astonished that it had been so easy to get permission from Sidi, but I also think he may have decided this a long time ago, and was just waiting for the right moment. So, pretty excited and content with myself, I headed into town with Maryam to make the copies. I had no idea that some serious challenges still lay before me.

When we got to the copy shop, the machine was out of order. So we walked to the next place, which took quite some time. When we got there, their machine was working, but they had no paper. So we went to another place. I was getting nervous, as I was running out of time. In this shop, where the machine worked and they had paper, I encountered still another problem: The teachings were written on lengthy, legal-size paper, and this place didn't have the right size paper. So we left in search of still another. By this time, I was anxious because of the time restraints and was wondering if it was worth missing the plane—or if I should just accept that the teachings were not meant to leave the zawiyah. Finally, after much searching, we found a place that had a machine and the right size paper. But someone was using the machine, and I had to wait. Finally, after almost having a nervous breakdown, I had time to copy about 100 pages before leaving; I had to get a taxi to Tel Aviv. I did feel a great sense of accomplishment, and those teachings were to be of immense help, because they allowed me to keep a material connection with Sidi.

In fact, many of the things I had copied were letters to and from beloveds, which later became Sidi's first book published in the U.S., called *Fruits From the Tree of Life*. My sister Amina, who has known Sidi even longer than I have, has done a truly awesome job of publishing all the teachings that Sidi has made available to us in book form. (See the bibliography at the end of this book.)

I certainly left in a rush. Fortunately, I had already packed my suitcase. When Maryam and I returned in the taxi to the zawiyah, teachings in hand, I had the taxi wait as I rushed in, grabbed my things, and embraced and thanked Maryam. I did take a moment to stand alone in the room in which I had spent so much time. As I gazed at the bed in which I had lain and the table at which I had sat and written for so many hours, it felt as if I had been reborn there, and that it was my birthplace now. So I knelt and kissed the floor in one final prostration, and I thanked Allah for bringing me here, and asked for blessings upon Sidi, Maryam, and his family and followers. At that moment, through Sidi's spirit, I felt a deep connection with the last of the prophets, the bearer of the Koran, the guide of all guides, our beloved Muhammad, may Allah bless him and all these holy people. I had come with a broken heart to this truly special place, a small room in a holy land where so many great prophets had walked.

I had fallen in love again, though this time not with a face from the material world, but with something far greater, which was to create immense changes in the way I would live the rest of my life.

There were a number of hassles at the airport, as there usually are, but I made my plane. Exhausted and exhilarated, I started the long journey back to my children, and the dramas with Nathalie still to be faced.

It would be years before the situation with her would finally reach some resolution. Eventually we separated and divorced. It took a while for me to come to a peaceful feeling with everything, but Sidi never left my side. I would call and talk to him often, constantly asking him if he would ever consider coming to the U.S. He would always say there was no permission from Allah, and that he had much to do where he was, but to continue to read the teachings and share with others the path of the love and the peace and the mercy and the justice.

One day, years later, I asked again if he would consider coming and, instead of the usual "there is no permission from Allah" response, he said *Inchallah*. I almost fell from my chair in excitement. Some of Sidi's sons were here in the U.S., and he mentioned he would like to visit them, and that maybe he could come to visit Santa Fe, since Nura, Tarik, Mu'Mina and others were here. I started looking into setting up a non-profit, so that we could raise money for his tickets. Little by little, things moved forward. I think Sidi has been here every year for over a decade now. Many lives have been changed through his love and his teachings.

Once, while here in Santa Fe, Sidi met Dr. Ibrahim Jaffe, who has since founded a school, located in Napa Valley; this school, and a wonderful group of teachers, have brought hundreds of people to Sidi. When Sidi comes now, he travels to many major cities throughout the U.S., and shares his heart with all those seeking to know more about themselves. *(Information on Dr. Jaffe's school, locations where Sidi visits, Web sites, how to purchase books, and a two-hour documentary about Sidi can all be found in the bibliography.)* We are also fortunate to have a beloved, and one of the leaders of the community, Fethi Ben Halim, almost always available to translate Sidi's teachings. Fethi has the extraordinary gift of being able to translate Sidi's words almost simultaneously as he talks and, through the translation, to transmit the essence and the heart of the teaching.

I find it a bit difficult to end this story because, in truth, it still goes on. For years after my first visit with Sidi, I continued to struggle and worry. With Sidi's guidance and the grace of Allah, I feel I have come to a place of peace and well being that would have been impossible to reach without him and his guidance. I live a quiet life now; and the following quote from *The Path to Allah Most High* sums up, better than my words can, where I feel I am moving and how I would like to live:

> *In the same way, if the seeker receives the warm breezes of protection, and the tree of his yearning becomes green and blossoms with life and flowers, he no longer has a desire to mix with creation. He is overcome with an affinity to the hereafter and concerns himself more with the rida (satisfaction) of Allah. The earth no longer attracts him; he prefers*

seclusion and retreat. He is fortunate if he has the guidance of a shaykh who is a gnostic of Allah who can show him the way to the haqq (truth). A shaykh, who is knowledgeable in tarbiyah. (This is a quality of the one who raises the child in the perfect way.) The shaykh teaches him the dhikr (remembrance of the name), so that he is happy in his retreat, no longer desires the creation, and sits in the khalwa (retreat).

My purpose when I started this story was to share with you, from my heart to yours, how Sidi and his teachings have helped me through many situations. I hope these words have helped you in some way, opened some doors, and given you ideas of how you can use these teachings in your life. I know that most of my pain, if not all of it, occurred because my heart was not open, and the love was blocked. Because I was controlled too much by my nafs, I was unable to experience enough of a connection with the divine of love of Allah, which is inherent in all of us. Love is eternal. It can never die, because it is connected to our creator, who is eternal. No matter what challenges we face in life, no matter how painful it may be—if we can find a way to express love, I believe we will be healed.

I hope you can feel how blessed I feel to have known Sidi. I encourage everyone who feels lost to find a guide. I don't know how many there are, but I do know there is at least one. I searched for many years, along many paths, through many religions, looking for someone who I felt knew God and could take me to God. One does not need to become Muslim to work with Sidi. But if you want the full taste, as I

did, then you might want to open your heart, to explore
Sufism and its essence.

In the years since my first visit to Jerusalem, I've spent much
of my life focused on studying and using Sidi's teachings. I
have a different life now, though I might still look like the
same person on the outside. I feel I've moved on from the
painful separation and divorce, and have arrived in a
different place. I feel my bond with my children is stronger
than ever, and there is nothing that can come between us. I'm
not aware of any pain around Nathalie. She has moved on in
her life, in the direction she wanted, and I feel positive about
how my life has evolved.

One thing that kept our relationship from working is that I
had trouble learning that sometimes people create on their
own, and at other times they co-create together. I was unable
to accept her quest for freedom; it did not feel like something
we were co-creating together. So I tried to suppress her,
which was totally unacceptable to her, just as it would have
been to me. I was more focused on what I wanted than what
she needed. As I was not part of her seeking anymore, I was
unable to accept that she wanted something different than
what I thought was best. My intentions were more about
getting my needs met than hers, and I simply did not find a
way that both our needs could me met simultaneously. As
divine beings we have such awesome potential, and we have
within us the power to really make our lives wonderful,
especially if we are prepared to accept the responsibility to do
so. Not only is there great joy in making our own lives

wonderful, but we can also find great joy in enriching others' lives. I currently feel immense gratitude for all that I have in life, and I want my heart to always be sending love and gratitude to Allah. I set a clear intention every day to live as joyously as I am able.

It took many years for me to arrive where I am now. I learned that divorce can be a real challenge financially, but God always provides what is needed, and the more one can trust and be patient, the more one can see the grace. I had to let go of virtually everything—not only emotionally, but possessions as well. But in the process I learned it's not the things we accumulate that make us happy or secure. It is our ability to love. I hovered on the brink of bankruptcy for many years, never knowing from one month to the next how I would meet my obligations. But it worked out every time. As I learned to trust and be patient, things slowly turned around, and I realized how much abundance was flowing into my life. I know now that I can feel love again, and that I am worthy of love—and I feel I owe this to Sidi, and all he has taught me. Just like a wound on the body, a broken heart can be healed, and we can all learn to love again.

When blocked love is released, pain is released. With love flowing through our hearts, we can feel aligned with our creator, and experience all the benefits that only this alignment can bring. I found all of my answers through Sidi and the teachings. But just reading the teachings is not enough. I see now that the greatest value lies in writing them out, and adopting them into one's life. I hope that, in some small way, the examples I've shared here have helped you recognize how important and valuable this is. If I can rebuild a life, then you can too—no matter how grim things look.

At times, I've felt like I've arrived at a point of truth, only to have another experience make fiction of that truth. Through the teachings, I've realized there are some truths that never change, and these are the truths upon which one can build a base that will not crumble. Most things that feel like mistakes are nothing more than lessons, from which we can learn these truths—especially when there is a guide to help. I don't think God ever takes you to a place where His grace cannot support you.

I am not particularly attracted to living in a way that takes me safely from one point to another, so that I arrive at the end of this journey in a neat and unruffled state. Yes, I want to take care of the gift from God that is my physical self, but I want to arrive at the end of this life knowing I have maximized this gift as much as possible, so that I can feel I gave everything I had to give. To make it to the dazzling light of the morning sun, one has to make it through the darkness of the night. I am passionate about learning how to bring happiness to others, about helping others help themselves. I find more value in yearning and longing to know Allah than in the attainment of things. I don't think I would mind arriving at the end of my physical existence, exhausted and spent, knowing I had done everything I could, and spent every ounce of energy I had, in order to know Allah.

We are just finishing winter here in Santa Fe. I remember feeling at the beginning that I was already looking forward to spring, though I could not see its promise in the cold and gloomy winter days. But I knew winter would lead to spring, just as morning follows night. I still have to take this on faith, and have the patience to wait. The best way of enjoying winter is not to complain, but instead find things I am grateful for, and continue to thank Allah for all I have. As Sidi says:

Be aware of Allah in every transaction with anyone. You show your honesty to Allah by being honest with people and in the work you do. Be straight with Allah by being straight with the people. Every living person is a child of Allah, and when you love someone, in truth, you are loving Allah. **Intimacy with Allah abolishes all loneliness.**

No one can move in this existence without Allah's help. Illnesses arise in a systematic manner due to corrupt leadership. Shepherds need to care for their flock. Let us pray that Allah leads them to the light.

Give love to everyone. Love created the universe, and it was given freely, without expectation of recompense, and it is in man's nature that the path of love and return to Him should be equally freely given. Divine love is a spirit without a body; natural love is a body without a spirit; spiritual love is body and spirit together.

Start now by finding things in your life for which you are grateful; let your heart open in praise of God, and let your love flow toward that to which you can—be it a child, parent, or sibling, or the fact that you have eaten today and have a bed to sleep in. Let your love flow. What is important, is that you open your heart.

If you feel lost, and anything I have shared has touched you, start reading some of the books listed in the bibliography. If you have already been blessed to meet Sidi, deepen your connection with him; if you haven't met him and would like to, connect with the people mentioned in the bibliography. Sidi always encouraged me to meet with others who love God, so I have listed some of the communities where you can meet people who follow this way. Even if you are alone, and are not near one of these communities, still reach out to these people. Each of these communities started in that manner.

When one person catches a vision and plants a seed, things can grow from there. Dr. Jaffe's school in Napa Valley is experienced in helping people feel connected, and supporting them as they walk the path. Classes are held frequently throughout the year, all over the U.S., in which people can learn about this path from truly remarkable teachers who walk in this way, and whose lives have been changed in extraordinary ways by Sidi.

Sidi has come to the U.S. every year for some time now, and tours throughout the U.S. each summer, so it is much easier to meet him now than before. And with Sidi's energy and Allah's grace, a large tree can grow from a small seed, and many can find shade.

In a book soon to be published (which, as I write this, has no title) Sidi says:

> *And regarding the pre-eternal praise of the Covenant,*
> *which is recorded in the cellular memories of human*
> *intellects, it consists of Allah's praising of Himself in*
> *pre-eternity before the existence of any creation. So when*
> *He originated His creation, He said "al-Hamdu li-Llaah."*
> *In other words, "Praise Me with that same praise which*
> *was declared in pre-eternity."*

So with each part of my being and, if possible, from my cellular memories, and with this primordial energy Allah has placed within us all, I send praises to Allah, with the deepest and most loving gratitude for His grace and guidance. And I ask that He bless my beloved guide with His infinite bounties, and that He keep him always in His shade, the shade of which he speaks when He says in one of the hadiths:

"The Messenger of Allah, may Allah bless him and grant him peace, said, 'Allah, the Blessed, the Exalted, will say on the Day of Rising, *Where are those who loved each other for My majesty? Today I will shade them in My shade on the day when there is no shade except My shade.*'" Book 51, Number 51.5.13: *Complete Sahih Muslim*

Allhumdu li Llahh Rabbil Al Amin
Salih, a poor slave for Allah

Information on Sufi School Events and Shadhiliyya Sufi Communities near you...

Sidi usually travels throughout the U.S. during the summer and fall months. Gatherings are held year-round in many of the communities mentioned here...

Shadhiliyya Sufi Center in Napa Valley
P.O. Box 100
Pope Valley, CA 94567
877-720-8143; 707-965-0700

There are currently communities in the following areas. You may obtain contact information through the above numbers.

Tucson, AZ
Napa Valley, Marin County, Los Angeles, Fresno and
    San Diego, CA
Boulder, CO
Atlanta and Athens, GA
Chicago, IL
Louisville, KY
Boston, MA
Washington D.C., Baltimore and Frederick, MD (and
    surrounding areas)
Detroit and Ann Arbor, MI
Minneapolis, MN
Albuquerque and Santa Fe, NM
Woodstock, NY
Portland, OR
Austin, TX
There are also U.S. communities in Iowa and Washington (state), as well as international communities in Argentina, England and Germany.

Bibliography

The following books by Sidi are available at this Web site:

http://www.suficenter.org

You may call 877-720-8143, ext. 13, to reach Hadia Tirben at the Shadhiliyya Sufi Center, founded by Dr. Ibrahim Jaffe.

You may also contact Amina al Jamal, editor and publisher of Sidi's books, via...

Internet at *http://www.sufimaster.org*
e-mail at *amina@sufimaster.org*
phone at 707-765-0904

The Music of the Soul
...an introduction to the teachings of the guide of the peace and the love and the mercy to the way of Allah through the religion of the unity in the Sufi way. This is the path of all the prophets and messengers. It is a very important doorway for any student to the way of return to our real life. It includes a detailed explanation the stations of the way, which are mentioned throughout *My Journey to Know the Truth*.

Fruits From the Tree of Life
...questions in the form of letters from students, with Sidi's responses

Conversations in the Zawiyah
This book contains conversations with and questions for the guide in his Zawiyah in Jerusalem from 1977–1986.

Al-Wird Ash Shadhuliyya
Along with the ritual ablution and prayer, this book primarily contains a prayer that is an exercise for the soul of students of the Sufi order, written by Ibn al-Mashish in the 13th century. Our Shaykh, may Allah be pleased with him, has unveiled many of the hidden meanings of this revelation. It is an exercise of deep spiritual importance and strength from the spirit of the prophet Muhammad (may peace and blessings be upon him) to the heart of his saint, to give light and knowledge of himself to all who would follow him in his way. It is the only piece of writing from the hand of Sidi Abd as-Salam Ibn Mashish that is available for us to study.

Spiritual Medicine and Natural Remedies
This book describes the medicine used by the prophet, may the blessings and peace of Allah be upon him, to heal diseases of heart and body, and prescribed to others.

Natural Remedies Supplement
...supplement to *Spiritual Medicine and Natural Remedies*, containing more remedies to various illnesses.

The Children Around the Table of Allah
This book is a collection of stories and sayings of some of the early Sufis, the people of Tasawwuf, who followed the

path of the inner knowledge of Allah, the exalted. They were patient and trusting, ridding themselves of the comforts and benefits of the material world in order to purify themselves and their hearts to live only for their beloved Allah. They persevered through the many difficulties and misfortunes they had to face in the annihilation of themselves. A profound explanation of the meanings of the names of Allah introduces this teaching from the lives of the friends of Allah. Two discourses from those early glorious days are also included: *Eternal Stopping Places* and *The Compassion of the Sufi*.

Deeper Meaning Behind the Pillars of Islam
This book covers the topics of unity, ablution, prayer, alms, fasting and pilgrimage, and offers a deep understanding of the true meaning of Islam.

Tafsir of Juz Amma
An explication and detailed explanation of the meanings of al-Fatihah [Q1] and of Juz Amma [Q78 to Q114] in their Shari'a sense and their Haqiqah sense.

Tafsir of Juz 29 and 28
...further explanations of the Koran

The Meaning of the Names of Our Lord
This book contains 99 names of God and their meanings. There is a hadith that says, "To God belongs ninety-nine names." While any two lists may add up to more than 99, any one list is limited to this number. The names are

revealed directly in the Koran, or from the meaning given
in certain passages, or they are names that are tradition-
ally known, but are not in the Koran. Some are derived
from the Arabic grammar of the names in the Koran, but
they are not widely accepted.

How The Arrival is Realized,
O People of Hearts and Souls and Intellects
In this book our Shaykh unveils the meanings of the
belief of the gnostics who know Allah by Allah. It is an
ordering and description of the stations and states of the
travellers as they disappear, and their abiding stations
come to naught until that which has never existed per-
ishes and that which has always been abides and remains.

The Splendid Garden of Truths
This book contains 48 discourses on the reality of
existence, and the soul as an image of life through the eye
of He who exists. This is the essence of all the teachings
that have come before it, and it is the station of the guide
of the Sufi way. May Allah keep and bless him always,
and his slavehood, and all this holy line from our master
the holy prophet Muhammad, may Allah's peace and
blessings be upon him.

The Meadow of Poetic Truths: Diwan of Shaykh Muhammad
To understand the teachings and poetry of the Shaykh, it
is necessary to enter his world, the world of the real
Islam—the religion of the unity of the Prophet
Muhammad, may the peace and blessings of Allah be

upon him, who brought the light and the mercy to all—
and to surrender to the light of the religion in the path of
the Sufi way that was taken by all beloveds who have
come before. This Diwan is presented to all his beloveds,
especially in this country, so that they can taste the secrets
of the reality and return to what Allah created them to be
from the beginning.

The Path to Allah Most High
"I say, calling upon my Lord and calling upon His generosity, 'O You who created the tree of the world and who
gave it the fruits of the sons of Adam and who chose from
among them Muhammad, O our God, guide us to the
straight path and make us steadfast in Your right religion.
O our Lord, do not entrust our affairs to ourselves, not
even for the blink of an eye. Bestow upon us Your gifts
and take us by You from us and grant us the gift of Your
existence in us. Make us develop in the ocean of Your
gifts through the constancy of the tajjali of Your jamal and
jalal. O God of all the worlds, by Your mercy, O most
merciful and by Your generosity, O most generous, I say
all of this as a reminder so that whoever wishes may take
a way towards his lord.'"

Stories of the Prophets
All 21 chapters of *Stories of the Prophets* contain teachings
and lessons for everyone, as the guide explains the deep
meaning of the life of every prophet with original
illustrations by Huda al-Jamal.

Prayer Manual
...a transliteration of the Arabic prayers

The Taste of the Love
A discourse on the knowledge and levels of arrival of the reality of the path of lovers and seekers of the highest divine light and beauty through tasting.

The following video and audio titles are available
at this Web site:

http://www.suficenter.org

You may also call 877-720-8143, ext. 13, to reach Hadia Tirben
at the Shadhiliyya Sufi Center, founded by Dr. Ibrahim Jaffe.

Truth of a Sufi, Parts 1 & 2

> Mystical film in two parts, sharing the Sufi teachings of
> Sidi Shaykh al-Jamal ar-Rifa'i, head of the Higher Sufi
> Council in Jerusalem and the Holy Land, and a teacher in
> al-Aqsa Mosque. Sidi is head of the Shadhuliyya Tariqua,
> and has published many books. These films share basic
> and advanced teachings, as Sidi answers questions from
> the hearts of students. Healing, music, relationships,
> work, family, religion, and love are just a few of the topics
> discussed. This rare film covers Sidi's life in Jerusalem
> and the U.S., and is one of the only films to ever have so
> much personal contact with a living master.

New Realities

Poetry & Songs

July Poetry & Dhikr

Al-Wird CD Recording

As-Salat, Al-Wazifa

Printed in the United States
34689LVS00002B/175-207

9 781598 000849